SATIRE FOR THE SOUL

This book will never be a
Pulitzer Prize Winner!

By

Ron Ruthfield

ISBN 978-1-960903-91-4 (Paperback)
ISBN 978-1-960903-94-5 (Hardcover)
Available as ebook

Copyright © 2023 by Ron Ruthfield

All Rights Reserved. No part of this publication may be reproduced, distributed, or transmitted in any form or by any means, including photocopying, recording, or other electronic or mechanical methods without the prior written permission of the publisher. For permission requests, solicit the publisher via the address below.

Publify Publishing
1412 W. Ave B
Lampasas, TX 76550
publifypublishing@gmail.com
email author @ rruthfield@gmail.com

Cover Design: Philip Gibbs

ACKNOWLEDGE MINTS

I thank a marvelous group of people who spurred me on to continue with my writing even though I'm not even giving them a free copy of this book. Of course, they won't know that until they read this after the book is published. Listen, you might think I'm cheap and that's okay, but I have a budget to meet, and my social security checks are being eroded because of our government's out-of-control fiscal policies. Nah, I'm just kidding. If you're someone mentioned here, then you really have been like a roll of tasty spearmint Life Savers, Tic-Tacs and Altoids and will receive a complimentary signed copy which will gather some dust because you're going to place it on a bookshelf and never read it. If that's true, then redact my signature.

Thane Rosenbaum, one of the great public intellectuals in America. He has served as a Distinguished Professor of Law at several major universities in the Northeast, a widely sought after public speaker, a prolific author, and a legal analyst for CBS News Radio. His comments have been inspirational and immensely supportive even though he wears funny glasses.

Dr. Floyd Stern, a retired physician, and despite his heavy schedule and commitments, gave me superb encouragement simply by offering his grin, after reading some of the chapters. I believe Dr. Stern mentioned that if I didn't need the money, I wouldn't have had to write another book.

Dr. Ronnie Loring, one of my go-to guys who is blessed with a great sense of humor and excellent commentary on my work. A true visionary which is why he became an optometrist. Many years ago, I thought about stealing Dr. Loring's bicycle even though it was manufactured for females. Dr. Loring offered me 25 bucks to include him on this list. I agreed but his check bounced after the printing.

Dr. Arthur Lane, a root canal specialist who, I know for certain, will ask me for 100 complimentary copies of this publication to hand out to patients because they're in constant agony from his dull drill and actually believes they'll read this book and get some chuckles. He also goes by the nickname, NoPainLane, which is like saying Torquemada, Spain's Grand Inquisitor of the late 15th century and early 16th century, loved Jews.

If you're fortunate enough to read this book but have been left off this list, that was done on purpose simply because I was running out of money to even get the book printed. If you'd like to make a large donation, I'll include you in the second printing even if I've never heard of you.

ABOUT THE AUTHOR

Ron Ruthfield

Ron Ruthfield is a former reporter for a CBS-affiliate TV station, newsman for The Associated Press, communications executive, essayist, and satirist. He grew up on Miami Beach where he attended South Beach Elementary School where he served as a distinguished member of the safety patrol in the 4th, 5th, and 6th grades and was awarded a special honor for allowing Dr. Stephen Hawking, who became one of the world's most foremost theoretical physicists and cosmologists, to cheat in class when he constantly looked at Mr. Ruthfield's test papers.

Mr. Ruthfield is the author of the fact-based thriller, The Capital Underground which deals with America's War on Drugs, the Witness Protection Program, and international money-laundering. He makes his home in a happy hollow in the Blue Ridge Mountains and every now and then walks around aimlessly pondering how he ever wound up becoming a hillbilly.

Satire for the Soul is one of a series of books which will have the same title but completely different content. We hope you'll begin a collection because they will be as important as your Family Bible, your diamonds and pearls, your financial legacy, all of which will go to your children, grandchildren and perhaps your ugly and avaricious cousins who constantly appear at your home at the very worst times like Thanksgiving and Christmas, and never help cleaning the table or washing the dishes.

FORWARD

Why I've decided to write a book at this time is totally irrational.

Full disclosure: This lexicon is a primer, a compendium of various subjects that I've been scribing since the introduction of two nefarious diseases, including COVID-19 and the near-fatal malady of social intercourse, not to be confused with an actual subject taught at Ivy League schools and 3,000+ other institutions, including mental, or anything resembling normalcy.

First, the world is still petrified that there will be another outbreak of COVID-19 or some other Chinese-produced or Russian-originated deadly pandemic. If you haven't heard of COVID-19 you're probably like many other sclerotic humanoids who ingest 100 mgs of Xanax, swallow a quart of Southern Comfort, and lie down on an active railroad track every hour. That should definitely lessen the pain of what the United States has gone through the past several years.

By the time you get to read this we might well be in our third or fourth iteration, or perhaps a vaccine that will kill everyone who agrees to have a liquid-filled syringe stuck in an arm, leg or buttock.

Penning this is a certain sign that my undisciplined lifestyle precludes me from finishing things on time. Or ever. Just kidding. Actually, I've managed to finish eight books, but I got tired of reading any more than that.

It's almost as though I was programmed and created in some foreign country's lab with a special assignment of authoring another book while in medical lockdown and wearing an assortment of insufferable mouth-and-nose masks and binging on Netflix flicks and television series in my bathrobe which, every 72 hours is thrown into a bleach bath in our washing machine along with white underwear except for the time I threw in red and blue underwear as well, giving an illusion that even my groin and backside are patriotic. All of this while my hair is growing past my fourth cervical vertebrae, which is why I've taken selfies of my head and sent them to all four barber shops in town for haircut estimates.

Second, I've reached the age of being considered a wooly mammoth, a milestone fraught with the inevitable danger and absolute reality of winding up in a marble orchard, without perpetual care, prior to completion of even one chapter. I've left strict instructions for my wife to locate an English-writing freelance obituary dramatist to conclude the tome or what I'd prefer to call my magnum opus which sounds much more elegant and much less ominous than "tomb."

Meantime, I'm making certain that we maintain our six degrees of horizontal separation from other humans, rather than being permanently housed in a hole that's six feet deep except in South Florida, where I was raised and where saltwater hits the tip of a shovel after a one-foot-dig. Besides, "social distancing" sounds much more durable and longer lasting than some graveyard rabbi uttering the pleasantries of finally reaching the gates of Hashem or whom you might know as God while rocking back and forth on a patch of manicured grass. "Pass the shovel, please" is not my idea of a hip going-away party unless it's accompanied by Errol Garner playing Misty in the key of C. (No Grateful Dead, please.)

And as long as I'm on the subject of death, I would like to have a closed casket funeral during which a three-piece band plays "Pop Goes the Weasel" while everyone stares at the bone box in breathless anticipation of a zombie event.

My life, being as perpetually peripatetic as it has, took its ultimate turn in 1986 when my significant other and I decided to look at Miami, FL, in the rearview mirror and, with our shaggy 14-pound black-Spaniel mutt, schlep to North Carolina, a step that would ultimately lead to a new sense of being and a sweeter joie de vivre.

I don't have the foggiest clue as to why there has to be a FORWARD in a book. What do you think readers do? Start reading from the back of the book? They move forward, not backward. However, if you want to start from the end, I'm definitely okay with that because it doesn't matter where you begin, it's where you wind up.

Well, here's something I can say about Satire for the Soul. Nothing is in order. Pick and choose what you'd like to read at random.

IT'S SATIRE! With a slight Jewish accent. Don't take it too seriously. Chuckle. Satire is supposed to be sardonic, humorous, somewhat capricious. It lampoons, it mocks, it's sarcastic, it's offensive, it's a pastiche of a melody that may not always send the right note to the reader. Indeed, you can expect a lot of fabricating the facts (some people call it lying which is fine with me, although I call it stretching the truth). Satire can also be a delicious verbal bouillabaisse of absurdity. But with all of that said, enjoy the read. I hope it gives you a sense of pleasure that might well bring a smile to your face. And that's a good thing in a world filled with more problems than a Ph.D. calculus class.

Ron Ruthfield

Table of Contents

BIDEN ANNOUNCES 2024 RUN IN FIRST PRESSER

What a wondrous day, this 25th of March 2021. It sort of reminded me of every other day this month; in fact, since the 20th of January in this, the year of our lord-what-you-know-whose-gonna-say-next-during-his-first-presidential-press conference while the rest of the nation ingests a sedative prescribed and dished out by their anodyne leader?

Did you watch President Biden giving his first presser? Wow, now that man can read English! Almost fluently. I must say that despite the change in venue – from the James S. Brady White House Briefing Room to the more elegant and much larger East Room of the White House where a gaggle of masked, cataleptic "journalists" were seated and spread apart from one another as though their COVID viruses were going to hop on the crystal chandeliers and when the bulbs got too hot they would jump on the head of the president – Biden looked so pale-faced an aide actually asked Chief of Staff Ron Klain

Ron Ruthfield

prior to the conference if he should quickly find a Wendy's Baconator so Hunter's dad could get in about an hour of cooking time that would make the president look more suntanned and cheesy.

I can only speak for myself, but Mr. Biden looked so yawn-producing that just watching him made me feel as though I was drinking warm diet water through a straw, paper not plastic or metal.

With avid determination to not blabber, President Biden delivered his highly anticipated spectacle as Commander-in-Chief amid a backdrop of a border crisis, two mass shootings, a pandemic, the economy, China, the Abraham Accords, the Senate filibuster, gun control, infrastructure, and the sex lives of Andrew Cuomo and Cardi B.

Although most of the issues went unanswered, the president did manage to field a number of queries, the answers to which were prepared on jumbo-sized white cards sometimes used by speakers and late-night TV ghosts instead of a teleprompter. But with a few well-placed printed admonitions to "FOLD HERE" the president was able to reduce the size to a more manageable 16" x 20" mini-poster mass, then cleverly put them on the lectern or in his jacket pocket and subtly snatch them from one of those two secret spots whenever Press Secretary Jen Psaki whispered, "YANK!" Amazingly, President Biden only stepped on his tongue a total of 39 times, according to my official count.

One of the more contentious issues between Democrats and Republicans brought up by one reporter concerned the ugly Jim Crow laws of the past, those that prevented the right-to-vote by millions of African Americans. "Look, man," the old

Ron Ruthfield

crow offered, "If it wasn't for my dear, deceased Grand Kleagle mentor, Sen. Robert "Whitesheet" Byrd, (D-WV), who became a civil rights giant after filibustering against the 1964 Civil Rights Act, we wouldn't still be fighting this 'un-American' and 'sick' Republican Party."

"Huh?" asked no one.

When queried by one journo if he was going to run for a second term in 2024, the president seemed certain that as long as he was still breathing – upright or lying prostrate – he would do whatever it took to keep the nation moving forward, adding, "Why'd you ask that? What'd you hear?"

He was also requested to tell the American public why gasoline prices have dramatically shot up like an unoccupied shack while avoiding the subject of his shutdown of the XL Keystone Pipeline, Biden said, "The reason gas is higher than before is that there's been a large, pent-up demand by the public to drive through the mountains listening to Barry Manilow's newest album."

I don't know about you but I'm really looking forward to the president's very next press conference in 2024.

Ron Ruthfield

A BUMP, A LUMP, A THUMP, A PUMP, AND A TRUMP

On President Biden's recent trip to the Middle East, the Commander-in-Chief set a new precedent according to a new White House policy, and it could not have come at a more appropriate time.

"Absolutely no more shaking hands," announced his newly installed press secretary, Karine Jean-Pierre at a presser prior to the president falling up the stairs on his way up to Air Force One or down depending on the camera angle. Jean Pierre added, "It's fist-bump time all the time and just in time to stop the further spread of COVID-19. Just think of how many lives we'll save by not interlocking palms and fingers but by merely bumping knuckles with one another until they turn black-and-blue."

(Apparently, Jean-Pierre hadn't checked the latest statistics showing approximately seven cases of COVID per week nationwide, far outpacing leprosy outbreaks in Liechtenstein.)

Ron Ruthfield

"Note that White House personnel with carpal tunnel syndrome will not be obligated to adhere to the new rule; neither will those who we urge to use their middle finger when speaking of diplomatic relations with Israel." An insider who has a close relationship with Jean-Pierre said she was referring to the entire Democrat Party.

Jean-Pierre pointed out to journalists and observers accompanying the president on his trip to Israel and Saudi Arabia – in the most profoundly balanced way – that they need to be aware that the American Israeli Public Affairs Committee (AIPAC) always has speakers at its annual conference who use "severely racist, Islamophobic rhetoric" and has become known for trafficking in overt anti-Muslim and anti-Arab while lifting up Islamophobic voices and attitudes. (Oh, wait. I believe she failed to mention that President Biden appeared as a keynote speaker at AIPAC's 2020 annual conference a mere eight months prior to his election as President of the United States. Whoops!)

And just like Jean-Pierre is the first African American woman to be the White House Press Secretary, Israeli President Isaac Herzog was the first international leader to be fist-bumped by Biden, a pyrrhic victory in the annals of the Olympics, Maccabiah Games, and International Diplomacy Competition sponsored by ISIS.

Standing next to Herzog, Israeli Prime Minister Yair Lapid quickly slipped his hands in his pants' pockets to avoid knocking his knuckles against Biden's. However, a U.S. Secret Service agent was overheard telling someone that Lapid could have had a sharply pointed mezuzah in one of his pockets but chose to avoid an international incident had he decided to use it if Biden forgot the new policy and decided to shake hands.

Ron Ruthfield

Not the same with former Prime Minister Netanyahu. Biden and Bibi shook hands like actual gentlemen, both of whom appeared to be genuinely warm to each other except when Bibi, a one-time Israeli commando, gently crushed Joe's right appendage with a grip equaling that of a crocodile chomping on an elephant. According to one reporter, a Magen David Adom ambulance was on standby just in case President Biden required on-site first aid or a trip to Hadassah Hospital.

"Eeny, meeny, miney, MO..." declared Biden with a broad grin on his face upon arrival at the Jeddah Airport in Saudi Arabia." Carefully negotiating the steps down from Air Force One, the entire White House team had a collective lump in their throats praying to Allah that its commander-in-chief doesn't thump down the steps and land on his hands. After all, he had more fist-bumping to do.

The first one in line for knuckle-breaking was an easy choice. As soon as he got to shouting out "MO", Mohammed Bin Salman, a/k/a MBS, the Crown Prince of Saudi Arabia, the Grand Poobah of Mecca, Salman the Sword Sharpener, Salman the Deputy Prime Minister and Minister of Defense, Chairman of the Council of Economic and Development Affairs, Chairman of the Council of Political and Security Affairs, and the quasi leader of the Tiger Squad of assassins – and these are only his part-time jobs – was getting more attention by the world press than when he had Jamal Kashoggi, a Washington Post columnist who had criticized the Saudi regime, murdered and dismembered in the Saudi embassy in Istanbul, Turkey.

Yessiree Bob, we only mix with the finest. But one has to give Biden a hearty "congratulations" on behalf of every American citizen. He actually got the Saudis to pump more oil to send to the United States, the amount of which translates to being able

Ron Ruthfield

to pump an extra six ounces of gasoline a year for your SUV, or four additional ounces if you drive a Mercedes. A presidential coup de gas if there ever was one.

Come November when the Biden Administration's domestic and international policies are crushed by a new national reckoning, Biden and his crew of faux American Jews who continue to negotiate – au contraire, beg the Iranians for a new Joint Comprehensive Plan of Action representing a potential national nightmare for Israel will finally realize that President Donald J. Trump actually accomplished more on behalf of the Jewish State than a few fist-bumps that disgraced his nation.

Excuse me, but I have to go wash my hands.

ABBOTT AND COSTELLO GO ROGUE

The governor of the Lone Star state, Greg "Bud" Abbott (R-TX), has announced that titanic Texas taxes will pay for the completion of a Southern border barrier virtually identical to the one that was mostly built via the order of former President Donald J. Trump – "a big beautiful one" – who was responsible for finishing a whopping mile-and-a-half of new steel fencing and another 482,312 kilometers of renovations to a crumbling, rickety, old fortification that resembles the Great Wall of Norway that separates horn-helmeted Viking-like warriors with Russians who wear big furry and funny-looking hats with red stars in the middle to indicate their love for Red Star Vodka, made in Siberian Gulags, with very slap-happy slave laborers who on a daily basis are allowed a bottle of their production, which surprised Abbott's assistant and first cousin of Lou Costello, Frank, a Texas Mafia don and bowling alley lounge singer known for his rendition of "Don't Fence Me In Without My Woman" in C major who in his steely determination asked in a highly unusual and mysterious

Ron Ruthfield

manner, "Who's on first?" obviously referring to an illegal immigrant tightly hugging the inaugural post placed in the ground in 1948 and has yet to be replaced by a sturdier structure which President Joe Biden said would not be part of the "Build Back Better Bonanza Budget" which most likely will get passed in 2099, a mere one year prior to the turn of the next century according to actuarial statistics undergirded by industrial-sized, prescient mathematics.

"Don't doubt our willingness to do the job that was supposed to have been done by the federal government," Abbott declared, claiming that the new 30-foot-high structure made from stainless steel donated mostly by binary women – who don't have the first clue what that means and neither does your friendly correspondent – who have recently visited their attics and storage units and have found 1.2 million metric tons of old silverware and teapots, mostly wedding gifts and from their 1962-1994 visits to England which, along with their concha belt buckles and silver spurs, will fortify the porous border. The structural engineers working on the barricade claim that citizens on both sides of the fence will be able to see through the openings between the posts just enough to be able to squirt each other with water pistols.

In a remarkably cogent moment during the announcement ceremony, Costello added, "Watt's on second?" referring to James Watt, the Secretary of the Interior during the Ronald Reagan (R) presidential administration. Watt, leaning on the second originally installed pole, is believed to have the largest collection of tumbleweed on the North American continent, except for Mexico and Canada.

Private landowners, Abbott said, will deed some of their land over to the State of Texas upon which a portion of the

Ron Ruthfield

new wall will be built. State officials claim the process of registering the deeds should take place in less than 60 seconds in a clear move that shows how welcoming Americans are to foreign terrorists. When Costello asked Abbott, "Who's on Third during the press briefing?" Abbott replied passionately saying, "I don't know."

The leftover, unused steel posts ordered by the Trump administration are now lying in neatly stacked rows near the Southern border and which the federal government has already paid for will be cut apart, according to a high-profile moon bat in the Biden Administration, and used as flagpoles for 152 nations' banners, except for Israel, and whose citizens are permanently visiting the United States. The flagpoles will be placed in front of the U.S. Capitol and utilized as a blockade in the event there's another insurrection.

In a surprise move, the White House has proclaimed that the administration will bequeath the leftover scrap metal to the president's son, Hunter, who has begun another career in abstract steel sculptures depicting the world's most famous drug addicts, to be auctioned at a charity event for the Fentanyl Drug Dealers Association of the Americas in Tijuana, Mexico, next Mexican Revolution Day.

Unidentified sources at the U.S. Internal Revenue Service say there will be a 22% income tax increase for all American citizens to cover the costs of repurposing the posts and buying the foreign flags, adding there will not be any penalties or additional taxation for Border Explorers or Undocumented Democrats.

Ron Ruthfield

AFGHAN REFUGEES PREFER HOLY HOLES SAY POLS AND POLLS

A Pentagon spokesman announced early today that a new poll taken by Pew and commissioned by the U.S. military-industrial complex shows that Afghan refugees are causing a big stink.

"It appears that many of the Afghans rescued by retreating American forces in Kabul last month are questioning their mandated use of standard military barracks' toilets or the type common to their homeland's plumbing system which consists of holes in the ground," said the public affairs officer at an unnamed U.S. Army base.

"There are critical times when even our own troops need to make rapid movements," he added. "The utilization of gaping openings in the ground in the event of an emergency simply doesn't give us enough time to flush any intruders out of our military installations.

Ron Ruthfield

"GI's have GI problems, too, but they utilize toilets that are either made by the Chinese or by Mexicans, the latter of whom are known for their craftsmanship in poop-and-scoop pottery."

The spokesman added that the Pentagon had assigned a propagandist to begin writing a serious work in Pashto and Dari to welcome at least 18 million more Afghans to America, all to be resettled in either Missoula, Montana or Del Rio, Texas. Called *The Love Affair Between the Mujahideen and the Latrine*, the 325-page book will be available later this year on Amazon in hard and soft-cover editions along with a free copy of the Quran. They will also be sold in supermarkets and at tables and oversized stools in Costco Wholesale stores next to its Kirkland brand of two-ply toilet paper.

An official for the Democrat Party voiced his concern about the unsanitary conditions in some of the barracks housing Afghan evacuees.

"So, what if they've already raped and molested thousands of women and little boys in our nation," remarked the Democrat from South Central Los Angeles. "All Americans, including Louis Farrakhan, should give them a fair chance to become acculturated into our society while getting complimentary memberships in Black Lives Matter."

"Headquarters has offered the Afghans the one-ply, 176-sheet Scott Tissue roll and the two-ply, 150-sheet Charmin but they continue to complain that neither meet their hand inspired standards, the spokesman asserted, which means to never shake the hand of an Afghan even if someone uses four quarts of Purell beforehand.

Ron Ruthfield

"Muslim tradition teaches that toilets are possessed by demons and as a result followers of Islam may be reticent to make contact with them because as we are taught, inshallah, the Devil plays with the backsides of the sons of Adam," remarked Dilly bin-Pickle, former Cultural Minister for Afghanistan who didn't respond to the question, 'Did Eve use leaves?'

Islamic teachings encourage squat toilets, or a hole-in-the-ground, and forbid men to urinate standing up. When U.S. forces were stationed at Kandahar Air Base in the southern part of Afghanistan, the toilets were segregated between American and non-American personnel, except for the British since they've always been considered worthy opponents in pissing contests.

"When the Afghans used our port-a-potties, they stood on the seats, then squatted which caused quite a mess. However, that does not happen here in the states where we are now serving the refugees a much more binding type of rice," the spokesman said. "Most of the Afghans we know have had crap-happy pappies, which is significantly more explanatory than 'I have to go use a hole in the ground.'"

BIDEN ADMIN SAYS CHINESE BALLOON REPRESENTS REMAKE OF FAMOUS FILM

In a statement released by the White House today, the alleged Chinese balloon which is now hovering around Myrtle Beach, SC, is nothing more than a redo of Around the World in 80 Daze.

According to the U.S. Secretary of Balloons and Blow-up Dolls, Peter Puffemup, there's a cast of six actors in the basket of the airborne vehicle. "However," added Puffemup, "there's a chance that if we are mistaken and the Chinese begin throwing lit firecrackers from the balloon's basket, I am admonishing the American public to take cover in their personal subterranean, middle terranean, and overground shelters in the event the balloon explodes and tosses the six bodies out of the basket and come close to landing on your head."

Ron Ruthfield

BULLETIN: It now appears as though the remake of the movie will be immediately halted. Secretary Puffemup has reported that the balloon has been shot down by people on the beach using peashooters and slingshots.

"I couldn't believe how much that balloon hid the sun," commented one uber-tanned swimmer. "I came here on a family vacation and couldn't believe they were making another film that I had seen on TV several times. And, hey, I didn't like the old one and knew I was not going to enjoy this one, either. The reason I watched it on television in the first place was because I was forced to watch it when I was in a Chinese prison camp."

President Joe Biden added that he wished the swimming public wasn't so mean-spirited by taking out the balloon. "Didn't they realize that six actors were aboard, not including my son, Hunter? For goodness sakes, man, those were probably Republicans who put the balloon out of commission. They'll do anything to anger the Chinese government."

Former Speaker of the House, Rep. Nancy Pelosi (D-CA), remarked from her Botoxed lips, "I could have torn up that helium-filled whatchamacallit with my bare hands if I had wanted to just like I did with Trump's State of the Union speech. Floating a big thing across the United States is a very positive occurrence for all of us. We need to learn how to live together in harmony. Yes, I once read that in a fortune cookie. Taking it out of commission with peashooters and sturdy slings violates the rights of more than a billion Chinese nationals, not to mention its operatives in the White House and Delaware. China has a booming cinema industry and we've now interrupted one of the best films they've made using the United

Ron Ruthfield

States as a beautiful backdrop. It's not just our country! It's theirs, too!"

An official of the Chinese government, Sum Ting Wong, claimed the balloon was one of the leading props in remaking the film. "We will not stop until we finish the film. However, it might take us 80 years, and if you know China and its people, we can wait. We are not in a daze."

Ron Ruthfield

LANCE ARMSTRONG, WATCH YOUR BACK!

Did you happen to catch the TV or print coverage of the bicycle tumble this Sunday morning near the home of President Biden's estate, the one at Rehoboth Beach, DE? On an asphalt trail near the ocean? No bumps, humps or thumps? With nothing in the way except his front wheel and a security guide on a bike in front of him, trailed by a coterie of Secret Service personnel on bikes and golf carts? On a blistering hot day but still packing heat?

Personally, I noticed the 79-year-old president's front basket was missing; the metal one he plops his newspapers in to make it easier to deliver the Washington Post to his neighbors who live near the White House and close to his other four multi-million-dollar homes which he was able to afford because of the money he saved up from his newspaper routes, including Christmas tips.

Ron Ruthfield

The fact is that the only thing falling faster than President Biden on a bicycle is his polling numbers. Poor fella fell about 39 inches from his normal cycling position thereby matching his 39% national approval rating. Fortunately for him, it might have been a blessing that his distance to the ground was a mere 32 inches.

The one thing I would have stopped cold had I been on the scene would have been to scowl at his entourage – including his Secret Service contingent – and demand that they stop laughing out loud. But one agent in a more contained persona remarked for the record, "After the president's 987 days absent from the White House in a year-and-a-half, something like this was bound to happen. The Oval Office is safe and, given the plush carpeting, President Biden can't even shag golf balls, let alone ride around on a two-wheeler, although we're fairly certain he has a hidden 10-speed mountain bike in the White House residential wing.

One of the agents – and I'm saying this with every ounce of honesty within me because everyone who knows me has no serious doubts about my personal dislike for prevarication and falsehoods – with a big smile on her face, suggested that they buy the Commander-in-Clod an Amish buggy with enough room to take the entire Cabinet for a ride out of town in the event there's an insurrection.

Note that this was the 42nd time since the well-balanced "Schwinn Man" has fallen since he began running for the highest office in the nation. (**Editor's Note:** "Running" in this case might be a bit of a stretch. "Shuffling" would be a more appropriate description. Additionally, saying the "highest" is much more precise because…well, you know…his son is

Ron Ruthfield

Hunter Biden, and who wouldn't be proud to call Hunter his son especially on Father's Day Weekend?)

An insider and top-level government operative told me there was a rumor that Secretary of Transportation Pete Buttigieg had suggested right after Joseph Robinette Biden, Jr., fell up the Air Force One steps three times in less than 8 seconds that the Commander-in-Clod should have been given an industrial-grade tricycle with training wheels similar to the one made for Hunter so he wouldn't crack up too badly.

When the fallen Biden was able to finally stand after removing his blue Nike-clad right foot from the pedal of the custom-made cycle, he immediately took the same foot and stuck it in his mouth, munching on his very sore big toe and telling the crowd – with all the vigor he could muster – "Man, I should stick with pickle ball unless I can get Congress to pass a $100 million bill to fund my own personal velodrome."

Pay attention, folks. The president is floating the possibility that he'll be taking six months off from his presidential duties to train for the Tour de France. Actually, that's less time than he's taking off now.

Ron Ruthfield

PRESIDENT BIDEN GETS DECKED

The Bicycle Playing Card Company has announced that in honor of President Joe Biden's 52nd vacation (matching the exact number of cards in a regular card deck) since he first took office 18 months ago, then falling from his tricycle and causing a boo-boo on his elbow, the company is printing a special Collectors' Edition of Bicycle Cards to mark the historic landfall.

"Because President Biden's cognitive ability might be one card short of a full deck, the company is introducing a brand new 51-card bundle called Commander Clodhopper's Shuffle," announced Jack O. Diamond, head of global promotions for the Belgian-based company.

"The graphics on the front side of each card will feature a photo of President Biden doing the Biden Shuffle as he makes his way to the presidential helicopter on the front lawn of the White House which is somewhat concerning considering he

Ron Ruthfield

was supposed to be heading into the Residential Wing to get his 19th hour of sleep for the day."

The reverse side of each of the cards will be a set of instructions for Commander Clodhopper's daily activities. "51 cards will be plenty since President Biden will be below the 50 level by the time he finishes his first term."

"For instance," his press secretary added, "the Queen of Hearts says YOU will greet the Queen as she arrives outside the White House. YOU will make certain that the Secretary of State brings her tea and crumpets promptly at 3 PM. YOU will bow to the Queen from the waist down unless you feel as though you're going to fall over and land with your face on her silk shoes, thereby causing an international incident. HUNTER WILL BE BANNED from the White House when foreign and domestic dignitaries and/or prostitutes are in attendance, which includes various members of Congress and the Russian Duma."

"This new product addition will be a reminder to those who may have missed seeing the president nearly wipe out his groin near the Delaware shore on June 18. It might also be a reminder for card sharks who do not want to play their favorite card games with four aces, considering the president's staff is consistently putting one up his sleeve when he's not looking."

Diamond continued, "We sponsor many events in the United States and for many decades have had the highest profile of any playing card manufacturer in the world. Americans represent the largest segment of our worldwide sales and they know our company rather well, especially in the Senate cloak room where there have been rumors for years that President Biden has lost a vast amount of money playing poker with money he received from Chinese and Ukrainian government contracts because he couldn't quite grasp, as he sat on the Cloak Room toilet, that a royal flush always beats a full house."

"We want illegal aliens and terrorists to know that as each one is arrested and housed in a federal slammer, one of their bonuses for breaking U.S. laws will be a free deck of Commander Clodhopper's Shuffle, especially while they're in solitaire (sic) confinement. Obviously, they need something productive to do while they occupy a cell on an overnight visit, which is now the maximum incarceration period, a policy established by Secretary of Homeland Security Alejandro Mayorkas.

The only card game that will be prohibited is Texas Hold 'Em poker which, according to Mayorkas, doesn't match up with federal policy of detaining those who cross the Southern border illegally.

"The big coup Bicycle has been able to secure, Diamond commented, is that we have also managed to create television relationships featuring many of our contradistinctive playing cards, and as a result we have already secured a position for President Biden, after he finishes his 9th term in office, as the Master of Ceremonies for Let's Make A Deal."

The White House correspondent for Poker Today asked Diamond if the jokers would also be part of the blue-chip decks of the Shuffle. "No," he said, "there are plenty of those in the West Wing."

Ron Ruthfield

NO MORE CHUNKY MONKEY FOR WEST BANK JEWS

Ben & Jerry's Ice Cream announced it will no longer sell its products in the West Bank or Jewish neighborhoods in East Jerusalem and has joined the Boycott, Divestment and Sanctions (BDS) movement against thousands of Israeli Jews and Palestinians, most of whom would rather eat hot shawarma than ice cream.

Israeli officials said the nation's citizens don't have to worry about the boycott of the actual ice cream cones, adding that, "I'm not trying to sugar-coat the situation but we have enough ice cream Cohens in which to put the dairy products and are producing many more. Even ones that are waffled."

A statement, released by the firm on July 19, 2021, has been interpreted to mean the company has gone bananas and is immediately peeling its inventory from supermarket freezers,

Ron Ruthfield

and recovering its pints of Chocolate Peanut Butter Split prior to its split from the West Bank.

According to the company's announcement, Jews and Palestinians living in Judea and Samaria will have to take a Rocky Road into Israel proper to pick up their favorite flavors and take them back to their kids.

"I love Allah Vanillah," bemoaned Mohamed, a resident of the Palestinian city of Ramallah. "I can't believe those two stupid Jews who started the company are taking away our eating rights! Fine! I'll drive to Jerusalem with my cooler if I have to and schlep home. My kids always loved the Mullah Mud Pie flavor. Their hearts were broken when they heard of this tragedy."

A Fatah spokesman stated, "Allah, peace and Reese's Pieces be upon him, shall take revenge by sending thousands of rockets into Vermont to make sure the company's cows are slaughtered, halal of course, and will never produce another pint of Cherry Garcia ensuring that flavor is never again eaten at a Grateful Dead concert."

An interview conducted by a reporter from the Jericho Journal in a Jewish section of the West Bank suggested that Baskin-Robbins, another American ice cream company founded by two Jews will increase its market share in all of Israel, including Judea, Samaria, and large areas of Brooklyn.

When asked what she thought of the move by Ben & Jerry's, Chava Fliegelman told the reporter, "Such an expensive and fattening ice cream. Feh. I never liked those two anyway, especially because they're from the same state as Bernie Sanders. He calls himself a senator? And a Jew? He wouldn't

Ron Ruthfield

stand a chance to get a seat in the Knesset or even at an ice cream café on a hot day in Haifa.

I'll stick with my Baskin-Robbins. Who needs more than 31 flavors, anyway?

Ron Ruthfield

HARVARD UNIVERSITY PRESIDENT MAKES BIG SPLASH FOR HAMAS

Israel's announcement this week that it is planning to flood 300 miles of tunnels in the Gaza Strip with water from the Mediterranean Sea has evoked some of the most humanitarian efforts to save the lives of Palestinians, many of whom would otherwise likely become permanent visitors of Davy Jones' locker, clients of the Neptune Society, or a division of the Nazi Party's navy seals.

The World YMCA, in cooperation with the World Waterpark Association, has agreed to give swimming lessons to Gazans who live in the tunnels. "We must make sure that the underground terrorists have an opportunity to survive the antediluvian swim fest by learning how to live with sharks, barracuda and Jewfish, also knowns as the Goliath Grouper, lurking in the murky waters," said the Right Reverend Billy Bass, head of the divinity school at Harvard University, whose

Ron Ruthfield

President Claudine Gay (her last name is not nearly a description of her love for Israel), has called for the eradication of all kosher foods in the university's cafeteria and – I swear I'm not making this up – bathrooms, including dormitories and port-a-potties.

"Each Islamist graduate of the course will receive a complimentary T-shirt emblazoned with I SURVIVED THE FLOOD," announced Gay, "unless, of course, they get harpooned by a compulsive swordfish that recently had its nose sharpened."

In what might be considered a supreme moment of unexpected yet spirited largesse, the President of the Massachusetts Institute of Technology, Sally Kornbluth, announced that despite her being Jewish and a supporter of Israel, she has given explicit directions to faculty members to assign students to fabricate the very latest in technology-driven water wings, thereby saving the lives of rapists, murderers, torturers, and imams.

"We must do something to save lives, even if they try to kill the infidels," Kornbluth remarked when she appeared before a Congressional committee this week. "I will do everything in my power to make certain our Muslim students and professors are the recipients of my carrot-topped, homemade gefilte fish – I'll even supply the horseradish – as a reminder that despite the potential flooding of the tunnels, there's always a chance that members of Hamas can catch a wave that will safely bring them to the top of the tunnels to rape more Israeli men and women."

In a moment of cogency and economic cooperation, Hamas leaders have signed a binding contract to purchase

Ron Ruthfield

100,000 two-person plastic rowboats which when manufactured will have features that no other boats of their kind have, including gigantic holes on the bottom of the vessels. "The rowboats will be fabricated by an Israeli company," announced Mohammed Deif, military strategist of Hamas and former Middle East Champion of Underwater Felafel Making.

A spokesman for the Israel-based SodaStream Company, which will be retooling its equipment for making the boats, said, "The plastic will be identical to the material we use for our international customers who own our machines to make various flavors of soft drinks with our gas cartridges – whoops! I should not have used the word 'gas.'"

Word has it that the color of the boats will be green, white, black and red, the very same hues that appear on the flag of the country called Palestine, which of course, doesn't exist.

When this correspondent asked Deif, "What if the rowboats sink?" the top-dog military man and ideal candidate for the captain of the ship, The Caliphate, responded, "Then Allah will appear in a Speedo bathing suit with a surfboard right in the middle of the Red Sea."

Inshallah, may he also drown.

Ron Ruthfield

AL-QUDS: MY FAVORITE HOLIDAY EXCEPT FOR KRISTALLNACHT

I hope you're aware of the upcoming Muslim celebration of Al-Quds (loosely translated it means, "Let's slaughter every Christian and every Jew in the galaxy except for Jews in Afghanistan and Libya which at last count had zero Members of the Tribe" and which is annually held on the last Friday of the month-long period of Ramadan. Which means that soon enough I'll be fasting which will take place in my kitchen while I rummage through the refrigerator and freezer.

You're probably familiar with Ramadan which lasts an entire month throughout the world which means I'm going to have to purchase two holiday outfits, giving retailers an opportunity to make up for the losses they incurred by perfectly legal means via left-handed lunatics permitting wholesale and retail smashing, shoplifting, looting, and laughing.

Why two?

Because just a couple of weeks later is "Nakba Day," which commemorates – hey, not my words but those of Yasser Arafat and a bunch of other holy folks in various parts of the world – the catastrophic destruction of Palestinian society and homeland in 1948, resulting in the permanent displacement of a majority of Palestinians caused by everyone except Israel. May 14 of 1948 by the way, came immediately after the end of the British Mandate for Palestine and the creation of the State of Israel in its place. "Nakba" was officially named and inaugurated by Yasser Arafat in 1998, 24 years after the pussy-cat tyrant spoke at the United Nations openly wearing a pistol placed gently in a holster.

And the crowd went wild!

Memorializing the "Nakba," with the economy in such a slouch, I'm going to try my best to purchase them at either Walmart or Ross Dress-For-Less. (If I were in Miami, you can bet I'd be at the men's department at Burdines in the Kendall Mall despite the retail chain's bankruptcy in 2005.)

My duds for al Quds will be a green jacket that looks like I just won the Masters Tournament at Augusta; white slacks to let the Muslim world know the absence of color plays well to an audience of loco and terror-hungry, demented pederasts; and a pair of red shoes that will patently shine well to an audience of Iranian ayatollahs whose blood lust will never be satiated.

However, I don't want to wear the same outfit a mere four weeks later to observe Passover. I might choke on a piece of matzoh.

Ron Ruthfield

BROTHER CAN YOU SPARE A LIME?

The Biden administration's fiscal policies have reaped a heap of bitter fruits, including a bunch of lip-puckering lemons, tangy cranberries, and tarty crabapples.

The pure genius that is behind the Democratic plan-cum-manifesto to spend $950 sextillion for infrastructure that includes building an interstate highway between Wilmington, DE, and Honolulu, HI, Democrat Party partying, and other social infrastructure such as buying 400 million copies of the latest fictional account of Critical Race Theory and donating them to everyone in Virginia, Oregon, New York, and the state of Washington, is "stunning" said Robin DeAngelo, author of a #1 New York Times bestseller White Fragility, who so far has made more money than the combined income of the African American neighborhoods of Baltimore, Detroit, New York City, St. Louis, Los Angeles, Chicago, Oakland, and 42 other cities, including Opa Locka, FL. The $950 sextillion, according to the head of the Federal Bureau of Prisons and Waterboarding,

Ron Ruthfield

will be extracted from at least five bazillionaires, including one from an expatriated American now living in a hut outside the capital city of Harare in Zimbabwe, my ex-mother-in-law, and the owner of the gallery selling Hunter Biden's paintings.

The domestic policy package, which some experts claim is larger than the Spanish Armada plus 1,400 container ships floating off the coast of the Dry Tortugas near Florida (which is as far as we know still a part of the United States although the president is considering bequeathing the dry part of the Tortugas to Cuba), is being negotiated by a startling number of warthogs, among other Congresspersons, to help combat climate change so that polar bears which are now starving cannot be eaten by the Inuit or half of China's population, provide universal prekindergarten based on the exact plan initiated by the Khmer Rouge in the glory days of Cambodia, and expand healthcare until at least 300 million Americans die from the bitter fruits mentioned above.

In fact, rumor has it that NBC will be so broke it won't be able to afford to feed its peacock.

Ironically, on the very same day that Facebook changed its name to Meta (which rhymes with Zuckerbucks and Build Back Betta depending on your pronunciation) the president boarded Air Force One to Rome to attend not the G-20 Summit but the G-19 knowing full well he's the 20th "missing link," an official, scientific term for a carbon-dated transitional fossil, also known as a Biden in a Bone Yard, whose mathematical and economic skills and savvy might one day add up to the Gross Domestic Product of 19 planets, excluding Pluto and Goofy, and who spontaneously remarked as he tripped up the aircraft stairs scuffing his dark-brown sandals supplied by his son Hunter's crack dealer, "That's almost a dozen!"

Ron Ruthfield

While in Rome, Biden, who considers himself a devout Catholic except on Sundays, Ash Wednesday, Good Friday, and Palm Sunday, plans to visit Pope Francis at the Vatican for talks about what some say are difficult and moral subjects, such as why the papacy is blessing the building of a Boys Town in a joint venture with Disney in an Alpine skiing village where priests just have to be priestly. Of course, the official agenda according to unnamed sources include the COVID pandemic that the Vatican and Archbishop Desmond Tutu has blamed on the Jews.

Then, it's off to Glasgow, Scotland, which sits along the River Clyde Barrow where Bonnie was merrily staking out a bank for them to rob, and a metropolitan area known for its heather on the inskirts and outskirts of town. The same unnamed official known only as Vinnie said that the President will be wearing a polka-dotted blue-and-white kilt and will attempt to simultaneously play the bagpipes and hopscotch, and at the very same time guzzle a magnum of Johnnie Walker Red directly through a paper straw inserted into the drilled hole in his COVID mask murmuring, "Hey, you know that guy...I mean that guy over there...oh, you know the thing...that John guy who I'm playing 18 holes with at St. Andrews tomorrow even though it don't mean a thing if I ain't got that swing."

According to a White House press official, President Biden is scheduled to go river rafting on Loch Ness in an unending search for Nessie the Monster, which has been lurking for some time to find a tasty-but-bitter American to eat for Thanksgiving. The same source claimed turkeys may not be available in the United States for the November holiday unless the Department of Homeland Security gets involved by forming extra-large turkey shoots sponsored by Butterball Organic Frozen Fowl. Winging it, DHS Secretary Alejandro Mayorkas

Ron Ruthfield

said, "We might even get some Wild Turkey to celebrate…heh, heh."

Whether President Biden can turn lemons into lemonade on the global and domestic stages is yet to be seen but the odds at a sports betting parlor in Las Vegas is laying 100-to-1 odds that Biden turns the entire country into one giant fruitcake.

Peachy. Just peachy.

Ron Ruthfield

THE "KING" IS PUTTING HIMSELF IN A PICKLE, BUT WHO DOESN'T RELISH THAT THOUGHT?

According to the White House Communications Department, the name of the Presidential residence is being changed from The White House to Burger King Palace in honor of President Biden's massive, continuous, and gigantic whoppers – by far the most by any president in American history.

"There have been so many verbal missteps by the president that we hired a Special Forensic Accounting firm to make certain the number of nuanced statements – OK, OK, LIES – uttered by the Commander-In-Chief were correct," claimed a whistleblower for the General Accounting Office (GAO). "The project was so comprehensive that a staff of 32 statisticians and

Ron Ruthfield

English-language experts stopped counting at 35,432 – and that was just for the month of August."

"Not since Aesop's fables about the frogs who desired a king or the boy who cried wolf have there been such outright contortions of the tongue," commented OJ Simpson from his home in Miami located just a couple of miles from Burger King University.

Biden, according to the GAO study, lip-fibbed more times than Lance Armstrong when the cyclist denied using performance-enhancing drugs after he won the Tour de France seven times. Medical insiders believe the reason for President Biden's lies is because he has fallen on his head while riding his bicycle on at least 50 occasions even while wearing a helmet.

In addition, Biden has said as a youngster he was raised in the Puerto Rican community as well as the Jewish community, which would be evidenced by his ability to speak fluent Spanish with a slight Jewish accent while eating in a Chinese restaurant on Christmas Eve. That's about as likely as his son, Hunter, dropping off another computer at a Delaware repair shop.

The whistleblower also claimed that the leader of the free world has told more untruths than President Richard M. Nixon, especially when Nixon announced, "I did not have sex with Bill Clinton at the Watergate complex" or something like that.

The name change of the White House has been cooking for more than a year, said Janet Yellen, Secretary of the Treasury. "Size matters," she said, "so I'm calling for a reduction in the size of the portions we'll be serving at the drive-through window we are opening on the east side of Burger King Palace. The contraction and the increase in the retail cost of the

Ron Ruthfield

Whopper by 90%, plus the shrinkage in size of all of our products, including the wilted lettuce, will literally add billions of dollars to the treasury. Add a drink and fries, claims Yellen, and the nation will begin to relieve itself of being in an overheated monetary jam, which will also go well on an order of our toast.

"We anticipate a grand opening of the Burger King Palace on January 20, 2025," noted the White House's Executive Chef, Patti von Berger, a former Taco Bell customer and high school cafeteria food server who promised to usher in President Biden's second term by claiming, "Special orders won't upset us."

Plus, ground Chuck Schumer (D-NY), Majority Leader of the U.S. Senate, will be on hand to personally welcome the entire population of Hamburg, Germany, for a special complimentary cheeseburger and an order of chicken fries dipped in oil made by Burisma. Travel expenses will be reimbursed, which will cost the U.S. a mere $7 billion.

"Okay, Mr. President," remarked the banquet manager for the Republican National Committee, Colonel Harlan Sanders, "Have it your way, but hold the pickle, hold the lettuce, continue your dementia but don't forget us."

Some political observers and haute cuisine restaurateurs note that if former President Donald J. Trump is elected for a second term, he will rename the Burger King Palace. One of the names that has risen to the top is The Magnificent Maga Eatery that will feature a kosher menu in an attempt to become even closer with Israel's Prime Minister Benjamin Netanyahu and to help further and solidify the Abraham Accords.

Ron Ruthfield

Netanyahu was contacted by an unidentified reporter while he was in New York this week for a sideline meeting with President Biden and an address he delivered to the opening session of the United Nations.

"You know," the prime minister said in a private interview, "just think how much a hot bowl of matzoh ball soup and a hefty bowl of hummus might help relieve political tensions in Washington D.C."

Ron Ruthfield

THE OLD PLANTATION AIN'T WHAT SHE USED TO BE

So now Aunt Jemima and Uncle Ben are gone with the wind. Stolen in the middle of the night from the grocery store shelves as sure as our very own American anarchists are burning Old Glory, and as quickly as Gen. William Tecumseh Sherman set Atlanta on fire in 1864 and watched till it burned to the ground.

One would have thought that exactly 100 years later, every American would have become aware that the Old Plantation ain't what she used to be, considering the first wave of Civil Rights Acts that became law in 1964.

But national reconciliation never became a reality. Don't ask why. It just didn't. Nobody really knows the real reason. Sure, you can read the drivel of so-called liberal and leftist historians or far-right swamis.

Ron Ruthfield

But if you ask me, although I wouldn't always recommend it, you'd force me into divulging one cringe-worthy name as the dialectic: Democrats.

While the Republican Party since the time of Abraham Lincoln and Reconstruction fought for the rights of all Americans (I recall at the time that Honest Abe signed the Emancipation Proclamation despite the fact I wasn't actually next to the inkwell or presidential desk), the Democrats were busy building their socially acceptable architectural model of the New South which included Manitoba, Canada.

That would include gentlemen of Southern Comfort building an organization called the Ku Klux Klan (KKK), a social club for happy and well-adjusted American families.

By 1924, in case you're looking at your calendar, the KKK had six million members – all Democrats – a number equal to the same number of Jews butchered by the Klan's Nazi brothers a couple of decades later. Or in other numerical terms, a higher enrollment than the entire population of today's Denmark.

And based on WWII history of the KKK, they were thrilled and delighted to know that not only were the Jews murdered (didn't they know that most Jews were fellow Democrats?) but Catholics as well. Nothing like equal opportunity misanthropes.

The grand history by the Grand Wizards of the Democratic Party continued to have African Americans picking cotton like their masters picked their teeth after eating a couple of cobs of sweet corn. A lot of dark-skinned Americans fled north on the Underground Railroad with maps provided by the American Automobile Association to escape the Democratic whips. Or made their way by buses and jalopies to escape the calumnies of white Democrats, many of whom wore their own bed sheets

Ron Ruthfield

and pillowcases with cutouts for their eyes, a fashion trend that has lasted for decades.

So, what did they find in the North? More Democrats without the sheets. They couldn't catch a break.

Neither could they catch one even after the so-called desegregation and school busing laws – all aimed directly at the Southern states and legislatures – were passed.

If you're north of 40 and have read a primer on American History, how can you not remember the popular names of the time? From Orville Faubus to the fabulous J. William Fulbright; from Lester "The Ax" Maddox to George "I Love Negroes" Wallace; and from Strom "Dixiecrat" Thurmond to Robert "Grand Kleagle" Byrd – all Southern Democrats and politicians who fought and sought to keep African Americans in the bottomless pit of the economic swamp.

And not surprisingly the plan actually worked.

So then how dare Joe Biden, the repulsive panderer, and the Democratic Socialists, condemn Republicans for systemic racism? Well, they can't. And they shouldn't. And if they had actual human brains, they'd be members of the GOP.

This is the very same nation that not only elected and re-elected Barack Hussein Obama. (Racist nations do not elect black or brown presidents unless they're in the Middle East, Africa, the Caribbean islands, or Lapland.)

Although the Islamist-Marxist Obama actually and provably went out of his way to foment race hatred, there's not much anyone can do about the vast number of urban blacks raised by uneducated single mothers whose goals are to either live off welfare or dabble in drug dealing.

Ron Ruthfield

Most of them never even heard of a Republican, let alone voted for one. They prefer to stay on the Democratic plantation just like their sperm donors and the sperm donors before them.

And when the time is right, they will burn down the nation until it no longer exists.

Ron Ruthfield

NOSTRIL CHECKS MANDATED FOR WHITE HOUSE EMPLOYEES, BIDEN'S DOG

A White House spokesperson known privately to be a former crackhead and mushroom dealer, which pretty much covers everyone in the president's family except his 7th grandchild, has announced that the mysterious appearance of cocaine this past week in the West Wing at an entrance near the Situation Room were actually the contents of more than 5,000 packets of Sweet 'N Low apparently stolen from the residence's pantry.

"We found the pink packaging rolled up like a giant ball that was tossed within two paws of Major's doghouse," barked the mouthpiece, referencing the German Shepherd who once served in the Third Reich's K-9 Patrol and who President Biden selected to be the Official Mascot of the Senate Tickquitoes Committee. He added that a U.S. Secret Service agent on

Ron Ruthfield

presidential detail found more than 175 unopened Sweet N' Low packets in the First Lady's purse she carried the last time she and the Commander-In-Chief dined at a Burger King near Biden's Delaware home.

When asked by a member of the Senate Ethics Committee whether the president's wife might be accused of artificial sweetener theft, the spokesman exclaimed, "As the case unfolds, the Justice Department has assured the American people there will be equal treatment for everyone."

"Nasal inspections will begin immediately," snorted the White House blowhard. "At the president's instructions, we've already called in a veterinarian to determine whether Major himself ingested the powdery substance thinking it was nose candy. Current information suggests that the sugar-loving pooch which at one time was owned by the infamous Mexican drug cartel kingpin, El Perro Grande from the State of Chihuahua, never actually ingested the substance, although one witness said that Major couldn't stop licking what looked like Gold Medal Flour from his nose for several days and appeared to be in a stupor while clearly attempting to replicate his owner's daily persona.

More than 500 rhinoplasty practitioners from Hollywood, CA, and Miami Beach, FL, have offered their services pro bono – which in complex medical jargon means "with bones" – and have agreed to take a gander up the nostrils of every White House employee to determine if any have a deviated septum or show signs of needing a nose job. (The physicians have agreed to offer government employees a 25% discount plus tax and shipping. Tissues are extra.)

Ron Ruthfield

A highly placed source said President Jocaine Biden has appointed Vice President Kamala Harris the White House's cocaine czar. Upon hearing about her additional responsibility, Harris, in a very sober tone, said "HAHAHAHAHAHAHA."

Ron Ruthfield

SHE TOOK THE GOLD AND I GOT THE SHAFT

With all of the chaos, madness, and profound and confounding troubles in the world, I'm inclined to believe the subject of this story helps alleviate your deep concerns about war, school shootings, teaching critical race theory, cancel culture, terrorism, political corruption, a dramatic increase in murder and rape, college campus madness, an out-of-control surge in anti-Semitism, the erosion of free speech, global elitists scurrying about while scheming to rule the planet, and every body's favorite, "wokeness."

I much prefer writing with a broad smile on my face as an exposition of a much more convivial social condition: Divorce. A nasty one. It is important to note this happy tale is categorically not about me, he, his, cis, binary, zayde, gender fluid, comrade.

Ron Ruthfield

Rather, it concerns an old and quite reliable friend, Dr. Sy O'Nide, an intuitive, incisive, prescient and accomplished intellectual whose analytical and doctoral skills surpassed his complete inability to live blissfully with someone from the "old school" or one of the many recently discovered other sexes which in this case has no common cause or identity with the greater LGBTQIA+ community; neither would he have been content to build a domicile in a tent city for the homeless.

Oh, no. His bride needed and prayed for a much more concrete and established upper-class existence.

But after decades of a poisonous marriage in the course of which Sy created a cash flow just a smidge less but just as sufficient and efficient as Elon Musk's, he was either ready to jump out of his window (although he could not have done much damage since he lived in a basement apartment), seek the advice of a defrocked clergyman whose only godly task was ministering to lapsed Catholics and Jews (for conversion purposes), or file for permanent extrication from his marital contract which he signed with a No. 2 pencil. Purposely. He thought it would be easy to cease, desist, and obliterate marital scourge with a pinkish, rubber school eraser.

Clearly, the Man of God was the easiest choice for dealing with reconciliation or dilution, and after meeting independently with Sy and his spouse the cleric was quickly convinced and rather thrilled that he had finally found the 2,000-year-old soul of Mary and Joseph's daughter enveloped in a fine-looking modern-day woman who no one had even heard of despite the rumors of a possible second virgin birth. Perhaps she was kept in a cave near the Dead Sea so that the villagers wouldn't know that her compulsions dictated the more-timely malady known as borderline personality disorder. One might easily throw in a hefty bag filled with a severe case of bipolarity to describe her ancestral line of behavior. Needless to say, the clergyman got buffaloed.

Somewhere along the way, her forebears decided to include crossing themselves whenever an apparition or icon insinuated itself but that was left for followers of her brother, the Official Son of God who was also the Holy Ghost of the West Bank, including Jerusalem, until 1964 when a group of unknown clans called the Palestinians arose to claim Yasser Arafat was, in fact, a member of the Lost Tribe of Giza Flats.

Mary and Joe's son was a little kid when he was blessed with gold, frankincense and myrrh. Gold, Sy knew about. The last two remained conundrums until they could be defined and authenticated on an Internet site.

The one thing Sy always said about his beloved was, "I married someone who knew the difference between a karat and a carrot." Unfortunately, he always left out the part about the Three Wise Guys actually bringing dazzling diamonds similar to the ones he paid insurance on for almost four decades.

$heila had a tumor-sized diamond in a white-gold setting that caused temporary blindness to anyone who shined a high-beam Maglite on her dainty hands; both of which were always-well-manicured and shone like a metal Indian chief perched on the hood of a black 1950 Pontiac Silver Streak.

"Somehow," Sy once mentioned to me, "I could actually feel them during my sleep. The filed tips were well rounded, especially when they were gripping my skinny neck. Every time I got that feeling of a near-death experience, I ran out of the house at breakneck speed that actually equated that of the Pontiac at full throttle."

Ron Ruthfield

Suffice it to say, $heila would have made a great guard at Gitmo or a coal-fueled railroad engineer for East Germany. Her breathless enthusiasm for life certainly would have qualified her to be the only certified and carbon-dated female member of the Taliban. She was like a kid whirling on a merry-go-round in a never-ending circle of missing the golden ring, although she had plenty of elegant bands around her petite fingers, wrists, and elegant nape; most sparkled with crispy and crusty diamonds, similar to those in every jewelry store window on 47th Street in New York City. She kept them in a thousand-pound safe, fondling them on her own schedule even in the middle of the night and continuously muttering how cheap Sy was.

Life's journey to $heila was like a Monarch butterfly's erratic flight from Mexico to Canada's Great Lakes, not knowing it had but a short period to live and never quite making the most of it because the trip was too difficult, too painful for her wounded emotions. Landing in an economy-size net would have been helpful, but who knows if she would have gently rested her soul enveloped in the soft comfort of the labyrinth of mesh or scowled at the displeasure of feeling trapped.

But $heila also had some extraordinary talents. She had an angelic voice to match her devil-may-care music sensibilities, played at least 87 of an 88-key piano on which she could knock out everything from classic rock to Johnny Mercer and could even handle Handel like she was the Messiah.

"I always had a decent relationship with women, even when I was young," Sy once told me. "I think that's because I always thought of them as strange creatures from another universe. I really thought that my marriage to $heila would be

Ron Ruthfield

one made in heaven, but it turned out she was made in China, the center of the knock-off universe."

Like the 14th century Janissaries of the Ottoman Empire protecting the Sultan's household, $heila stood guard with her arms folded for hours at a time on the front steps of the symmetrical mansion in which she and Sy lived, thereby violating her parole from sanity as she searched for nematodes in the grass on the side of the steps. Or perhaps she was looking for a burial plot that she could dig up quickly.

Finally, it was time. It got to the point at which Sy would have preferred defenestration rather than staying married. After forty years of conjugal felicity, the chance of Sy staying in the marriage was just about the same odds as Barack Hussein Obama running for Prime Minister of Israel. To $heila, marriage was a word. To Sy, it was a sentence.

"$heila used to tell me," Sy claimed, "that you must understand the whole of life, not just one little part of it. That is why you must read, that is why you must look at the skies, that is why you must sing and dance, and write poems and suffer and understand, for all that is life."

"Suffering is my goal," Sy responded, thinking that would give her the opportunity to continue her objective of making me matrimonially deceased." It worked.

"I found out after I dashed out of the house one time that these words were actually spoken by Jiddu Krishnamurti who bounced on and fell off eastern philosophical walls like a New Delhi Humpty Dumpty. By the end of his 90 years of life he decided, much to the chagrin of some of his followers, that no one should follow his beliefs because, according to him, 'I maintain that truth is a pathless land, and you cannot approach

Ron Ruthfield

it by any path whatsoever, by any religion, by any sect...Truth, being limitless, unconditioned, unapproachable by any path whatsoever, cannot be organized; nor should any organization be formed to lead or coerce people along a particular path.'"

"Had I known $heila was an adherent to Jiddu's basic beliefs and almost identical to those of Ayn Rand, I would have shrugged and asked my wife to change her name to Atlas so she could cope with the weight of the world on her shoulders," Sy sighed.

Metaphysically speaking, $heila never quite understood how and why the world works as it does similar to the way she could never quite grasp the subject of marital anarchy, in which she engaged (scratch "engaged") daily. What other spouse would have sprinkled her husband's food with a white substance even while they were dining out? Once, during a sobering moment, Sy asked her about the powdery potion. She claimed she was trying to balance Sy's energy; Sy claimed she was attempting to translocate his body.

Sy made an appointment to see an attorney while $heila responded to an ad in the local paper whose headline read, "One less bell to answer, one less egg to fry," a perfect tune by a slick divorce attorney who had an even slicker ad agency.

According to my good friend, the split was rather amicable and met all the guidelines and policies set forth in the Affordable Divorce Act, a bill passed by Congress during the Obama Administration and made retroactive to the day before the American Civil War began in the event there were any leftover combatants.

"The one great thing that came out of this episode of my life," said Sy, "is that while we were walking out of the courthouse for the last time, $heila, who walked away with 80% of our assets, suggested I get myself one of those penis enlargers, which I did. She's 24 and her name is Brandy."

Ron Ruthfield

SENATOR SPOTTED SHOPPING AT PENNSYLVANIA THRIFT STORES

John Fetterman, the U.S. Senate's fashion consultant and lawmaker, was spotted at two chic thrift shops in Pottstown, PA, allegedly looking for a couple of polyester leisure suits, white patent leather shoes and matching belt, plus some leftover Hawaiian shirts worn by former President Barack Obama at a Maui luau while on a Democrat Party junket.

Senate Majority Leader Chuck Schumer (D-NY) confirmed a rollback of the upper chamber's dress code last week and the move was quickly dubbed the "Fetterman Haute Couture Law" because of the Pennsylvania senator's penchant for wearing hand-tailored, elegant-but-stained hoodies, sheets made into shirts, and saggy baggy shorts.

Rumor has it that Fetterman is believed to be partially brain damaged, a direct result of a lobotomy performed by Captain Hook, and likes to shop in Pottstown because of his

Ron Ruthfield

love for cannabis, especially while studying 4,000-page senate bills and resolutions while dressing in his usual garb of various colored hoodies emblazoned with "This Guy Has Chutzpah" and pantaloons well-below ankle-length shorts he picked up last year at the Paris Fashion Week.

Unfettered, Fetterman told the press at that time that he bought them in eight different colors, including Barbie pink.

Casual observers also noted that the senator shaves his legs.

According to the Pottstown Goodwill store's operations manager who was speaking off the record, Fetterman (D-PA) spent a total of $28.50 (plus a 20% Value Added Tax) for part of his new wardrobe to comply with the bipartisan resolution this week to make certain that senators, instead of dressing like shlubs, maintain the dignity of the chamber. The House is considering the same type of resolution but is having a difficult time because Rep. Gerald Nadler (D-NY) cannot find pants with a 64-inch waistline.

"I didn't realize when I was in France last year that the Salvation Army has a bargain shop within walking distance of the Eiffel Tower, thank goodness, which I serendipitously discovered right behind the French Foreign Legion recruiting trailer," Fetterman intoned. "Buying my tennis sneakers there, although lightly and slightly used, along with running shoes that only participated in six marathons, represents one heck of a savings.

"Those Frenchies not only provide us with their cabernet sauvignon, berets and three different size poodles," articulated Fetterman, "but as most citizens of the world are aware they also paid tribute to America by designing, constructing, and

Ron Ruthfield

installing the Statue of Liberty in New York Harbor 99 years ago. Or was it New Jersey?"

After Fetterman finished shopping at Pottstown's Goodwill and spending most of his clothing expenses for the year, he headed to the Second Chance Boutique where he was overheard asking the store owner, "I'm looking for a nicely kept loincloth to wear on the Senate floor. Got anything that'll fit me?"

"Senator," remarked the owner upon recognizing Fetterman, "The only thing I believe I have in my inventory that will fit you is a size 24 hat."

Ron Ruthfield

THE FLORIDA FELONS' FESTIVAL

A set of guidelines for ex-convicts to be able to vote in Florida elections have been released by former New York City Mayor and presidential candidate, Michael Bloomberg.

According to Bloomberg spokesman Vito Salmonella 32,000 former prisoners who actually reside in the Gunshine State will have an opportunity to cast their ballots because their financial debts have been paid and fully settled. Those include accumulated court costs, obligations to victims they raped and/or killed, and to snitches they beat up and plunged a shiv into while incarcerated.

Salmonella did not say whether the former desperadoes had to be dead or alive, although he indicated that some shovels would be used in what he called Operation Big Dig.

"Da $16 million Mayor Bloomberg has raised to pay doze fiskil responsibilities will be delivered direkly to da former yardbirds by the 67 Florida sheriffs or trustees in da county jails," Salmonella added.

Ron Ruthfield

"Doze samoleons, named after my own Sicilian family, will go a long way into makin' soitin dat da elekshuns are fair and balanced, not to menshun doze 32,000 votes will go to my pal, Joey."

Partnering with The Big Apple's former leader in raising the "samoleons" were the Open Society Foundation and the Tides Foundation plus a number of their affiliates, all funded by George Soros, a well-known political activist who always makes a definitive effort to display his doctrine of "democracy in action" and consume 32-ounce cups of Coca-Cola with a paper straw.

This reporter was given a list of first names and phone numbers throughout Florida, identifying by first-name-only some of those who have already been cleared to regain their voting rights, and given permission to get reaction by some of those who were locked up for various criminal activities and are now eligible to vote.

"Finally, after all these years, I finally can cast my ballot for a real live presidential contender instead of casting my knife into a corrections officer's belly," one of them declared. "Hey, she deserved it! She wouldn't even get me an extra 100 Grand chocolate bar before I went to sleep," the male ex-con told me. He also told me he plans to vote for Al Gore.

Imprisoned for more than 25 years, one of them told me he was sentenced unfairly and was happy to have been released after serving five years. "Simply because I raped eight nuns doesn't mean I had bad habits," he confessed. "They should have known better than to leave the convent's front door unlocked at a time when I was under a lot of stress. Even Biden, who's Catholic, understood it was only eight of them, for God's

Ron Ruthfield

sake." Well into the conversation, he mentioned he was considering moving to either the Vatican or Delaware to enter the priesthood after the 2020 presidential election.

After repeatedly calling one of the phone numbers of a convicted Ponzi schemer who had been given a 50-year sentence for ripping off more than $1.5 billion from "investors," I was told personally by Salmonella he was put into the Witness Protection Program in 2009 and was last seen partying at a Las Vegas casino with OJ Simpson.

Thank goodness Ted Bundy is no longer with us.

Ron Ruthfield

HAMAS FLIPPING OUT OVER ISRAELI DOLPHIN TRAINING

It has become abundantly clear to Middle East observers that Israeli intelligence agencies appear to be impeding Gaza Frogmen, also known as Toadies, from carrying out their Military Maneuvers and Missions (listed as 3M on the New York Stock Exchange) in the coastal waters of the Mediterranean Sea.

"We have captured a heavily armed dolphin by the name of Uzi who was trained by Israeli-American and former Florida Seaquarium terrorist Dr. Marlin Fishbein," claimed Ahmed bin Tunah from his Al-Qassam Brigades' resort headquarters in Nassau, The Bahamas. "We're sure that Fishbein is behind this contretemps considering his and other Jews' vicious treatment of Palestinian manatees which have occupied the waters, including Florida's Crystal River, belonging to the Palestinian people for thousands of years, including 1948.

Ron Ruthfield

"We know the dolphin's name is Uzi because it was on his military dog tag," bin Tunah said from his Paradise Island yurt decorated in the colors of the Palestinian flag, including blood red.

Bin Tunah, who rose from being a simple Gaza fisherman to simply a Gaza simpleton so that he, in his own words, can continue to help liberate his Toadies and other aquatic life from the "oppressed people of the Middle East, including Miami Beach, Key Biscayne, and Opa Locka."

Unofficial sources in Israel say bin Tunah (his friends call him Charlie) has often been spotted swimming in multi-hued foot flippers to the Florida coast where he has endlessly searched for Dr. Fishbein in an effort to perform a stealth-like shark attack against one of the leading scientists whose greater purpose for porpoises is a dramatic increase in their population.

Bin Tunah claimed, "Yehudi dolphins have been programmed to intercept our efforts to bring Fishbein to justice at the International Criminal Court in The Hague on charges of exploiting sea life, including mermaids and plastic from six-packs of beer."

"The Zionist interlopers have actually outfitted these gentle mammals (**Editor's Note:** Not the Palestinians but the dolphins), with a harness that fits the snout of the ocean-going, tropical-water animals and have attached low-grade nuclear weapons to their fins. They have been trained in the event they need to suddenly leap 25-feet into a suicide mission which has been enthusiastically supported by applauding audiences," bin Tunah said, adding that it's "the same height of the building rooftops from which we toss those evil Jews, gay men, lesbian women, and an assortment of non-believers. To the ground. On

Ron Ruthfield

their heads. As the Quran proclaims it is of benefit to all mankind and dolphins."

As of today neither the Mossad, Shin Bet, nor the Israel Defense Forces have issued a statement of responsibility about what could turn out to be a grand-but-nefarious operation geared toward what the Al-Qassam Brigades, the military arm of Hamas, has admitted could ignite a conflict never before seen on such a large scale, although anyone who's ever seen or touched a dolphin knows they don't have scales unless they're being weighed on one.

In 2015, there was a similar report in the Jerusalem-based Arabic-language Al-Quds newspaper with a circulation of 18 because – I swear, the editor himself told me this with his right hand on the Quran – "99.8% of Palestinians don't like to read and hate getting ink on their fingers."

At the time, an Israeli spokesman denied the story and in the spirit of traditional Palestinian values the readers burned down the newspaper's building.

Ron Ruthfield

GEORGIA OFFICIALLY CHANGES ITS STATE FRUIT

Officials of the Georgia Tourism and Development Department have formally changed its well-known sobriquet from the Peach State to the Fruitcake State, according to Fuzzy Pitts who for the last 25 years has what most Georgians considered a plum job.

"After what has just transpired in our senatorial elections, we believe that 'Fruitcake' is a much more accurate description of the typical Georgia voter and peach cruncher," Pitts said.

A member of the Georgia legislature's agricultural sub-committee, Rep. Alberta Cling, Baroness of Appling County, has already introduced a bill that calls for the total destruction of statuary honoring the mighty peach and eliminating the slightest mention of the fruit in all history books beginning at the kindergarten level and moving right along to post-doctoral research theses.

Ron Ruthfield

"It's only proper that we cancel the fruit, similar to the fall of Icarus as we raise up the lonely fruitcake which actually has a rich history in Georgia, specifically in Claxton, a city between Savannah and the sweet-tasting onion-growing town of Vidalia. We toyed with the idea of changing the moniker to the Pecan State but it starts with 'P' and contains four letters used to spell Peach. We knew it wouldn't stand a chance, not even on our roadside stops like Stuckey's."

"In addition, the Claxton Bakery Co. is known internationally for creating one gigantic fruitcake each year which is shipped to one large family in a little home on the prairie who hate the product, keep it in its bountiful wrapping, but then bequeath it to another family until it makes its way to almost every family in America including orchard owners until it reaches the 200 millionth clan who finishes it off faster than Jon Ossoff beat Kelly Loeffler.

Rep. Cling also announced that the name of Peach County will be eliminated, bringing the total count of Georgia counties to 158, still the most of any state west of Bhutan. After the county's residents are evacuated the land will be set aside as a holy burial ground for Georgians who have contributed to humanity, including former Governor Lester "Ax Handle" Maddox; Wayne Williams, the Atlanta serial child killer; and Eric Rudolph, the 1996 Olympics bomber.

Atlanta Mayor Keisha Lance Bottoms and Gov. Brian Kemp, according to reliable sources, will be changing every street name in the state and capital city with the word Peach in it. For example, Peachtree Street will become Fruitcake Lane; Peachtree-Dunwoody Road will be known as Fruitcake-Dunwoody Drive, Peachtree Circle will be altered to Fruitcake

Ron Ruthfield

Boulevard; Peachtree City will morph into Fruitcake Village, and so on.

"The peach has been a deep part of our history – even long before there was a Georgia," said Goldie "Oldie" Paperman, Georgia's Fruit and Vegetable Archivist. "Franciscan monks introduced peaches to St. Simons and Cumberland Islands way back in the 1600s, just a couple of years after Jimmy Carter was born. In fact, a Columbus planter Raphael Moses was marketing peaches in the mid 1800s. And now that we have a U.S. Senator and Baptist minister named Raphael Warlock – um, Warnock – is that not a totally remarkable and wonderful coincidence?" Hah, hah, hah, oy vey.

But preaching the gospel in Georgia is one thing. Having this particular senator/minister sermonizing to the country is quite another. Before we know it, millions of Americans will be addicted to the Fruitcake and the bitter-lemon lessons of Marxist-inspired liberation theology that actually took root in Vladimir Lenin's vegetable garden disguised as red pepper.

Good luck, Georgia Fruitcakes. We hope that sometime in the future you'll get back your reputation as a perfectly healthy edible. You might even want to settle for being called Georgia Coconuts.

Ron Ruthfield

REPUBLICANS CONTEST PRESIDENTIAL ELECTIONS BY TERRORIZING NEIGHBORHOODS

Elected GOP officials, top-level operatives, and party members have committed massive theft and have wreaked havoc upon American hamlets, towns and cities because of the loss of the presidency to Democrat and former Vice-President Joe Biden.

"Stop the madness!" exclaimed the mayor of Mikveh City, TN, after a police department spokesman in his jurisdiction told hizzoner that a teen-age Boy Scout was caught helping an elderly woman cross Main Street when she suddenly got blindsided by a Biden-For-President sign that had blown off someone's front lawn during a windstorm and whacked her in the head.

Ron Ruthfield

According to a hospital spokesman, the woman is in stable condition with cuts and bruises to her scalp and ego.

"This is no time for political violence," Mayor Dewey Haitem admonished the townspeople via an immediate Zoom hook-up to the 312 citizens. "Scouts Lives Matter should've known better than to put dear 'ole Misses Pelosi in danger. That woman has been volunteering with the Women's Police Auxiliary for more than 40 years. This has to stop!"

Just outside Tuchas Junction, TX, officials said the Republican Party of Cheek County officially sponsored a toilet paper roll along every major highway and street leaving only the cardboard tubes for people to deal with. Sources said each square on the square sheets had a photo of Sen. Kamala Harris with a smaller inserted picture of former San Francisco Mayor Willie Brown.

"It was crystal clear the rolls had been stolen from the local novelty and magic store, Dirty Tricks," said Sheriff Tokyo Sayonara, the first heterosexual Japanese-Shinto-Samurai-American female sheriff elected in the U.S., a historic achievement. "One of my deputies caught three White kids with the wrapping paper hanging out of the back of their jeans. No wonder our nation's in the crapper."

According to Sen. Chuck Schumer (D-NY), "These acts of violence and vindictiveness indicate we need to bring tough measures against these vile criminals. In fact, Black Lives Matter and Antifa are already assembling in major cities to make sure that peace and quiet return to the streets of every city in the nation, and that Jussie Smollett receives justice."

Ron Ruthfield

The senator added, "Smollett is innocent. Everyone knows that." Except Jussie Smollett who, thankfully, is now behind bars.

Good call, Schumer, good call.

THE JEWISH TAKEOVER OF AMERICA

With apologies to Hamlet, "To be or not to be...a Jew. Let me count the oy veys."

Yes, there are millions of them spread throughout the land, both kvetching and kvelling about which new cabinet members and Biden appointees are really *Jews* (as in "*authentic*" Jews). Certainly, we know that Torquemada, the Grand Inquisitor of Spain in 1492, had a bissel Jewish ancestry but would we actually accept him into our shul, synagogue, temple, or yoga group? Of course not. And now that we're so well adjusted to having many high-profile Jews at the helm of government agencies and staff positions, should we blindly accept all of them into our farrago of Yidlach just for the zeitgeist?

Well, let's examine that desultory question.

Ron Ruthfield

Many fellow tribesmen know that President Trump's administration has been overflowing with milk-and-honey Jews who we will NOT review because if you don't know them by now, you'll forget them right after you read the master list.

One note to consider is that most fellow Members of the Tribe still think that Larry Kudlow, the president's Chief Economic Adviser, is Jewish. Sadly, he gave up his right to call himself "Jewish" or "Jew" or anything approximating the notion of being a tribal collectivist. Uh-uh. Now a Catholic, Kudlow follows a stream of consciousness that befuddles most American Jews, including me. Although I must say the Pope does have some awesome looking kippot (skull caps), and I especially love the Cardinals' red ones. Sadly, Kudlow no longer qualifies in making the Yid list.

Avril Haines. Her mother's maiden name was Rappaport, which in English translates to "If I'm not Jewish, I have some major explaining to do." Happily, Avril is a Jewess brainiac. Which is why she's been tapped as Director of National Intelligence (some Jews call it Natural Intelligence). Just think. It could have been Susie Rice but alas, not a Jewish lass, thank G-d. Now, if we could collectively just get Avril to change her name to Esther and believe in Israeli sovereignty that would make the transition a whole lot easier.

Ron Klain. What can I say – or should I say – about the incoming Chief of Staff? If I call his office, I've been wondering if he'll send me a White House golf shirt and matching cap at 50% off? If so, I'll buy the entire inventory of Trump gear and resell it at regular price at a local flea market. I'd also like to inform him I'm a fellow tribesman (I'll emphasize that he and I have the same first name and hope he'll admit his Hebrew name is Yerachmiel) but only if I can get a bigger discount.

Ron Ruthfield

I encourage all of us to give the newly appointed (but not yet anointed) Secretary of State a Wink and a Blinken and a Nod, although that might be a difficult task for some considering Antony Blinken's affinity for being a noodge when it comes to Israel. Blinken's background is SO-O-O-O Jewish that if I'm ever invited to one of his D.C. dinner parties, I'd be happy to play and sing the plucky tune, Mayn Shteleh Belz. A real hit, that one, especially for the many Jewish members of the Biden clan unless they're in prison. It'll bring down the Blair House, most recently re-designed by Mendel, Mesick, Cohen Architecture. Shh-hh-hh, that's still somewhat of a secret.

And who could possibly leave the subject without mentioning the return of Aunt Janet Yellen, which rhymes with kvellin', counting out and adding up the shekels. That woman is a shayne froy and real joy. An American zeeskeit and more of a Mamala than Kamala. More Jewish and more American than the rabbi in Boone, NC.

Now, the Grand Prize is a surprise. On the short list to be nominated for Director of the Central Intelligence Agency is Darrell Blocker, a Jew. Yeah, I know I know. There have been a couple of other Jews who have headed up the furtive activities of the U.S. version of the Mossad. But not this particular hue of Jew. He's an African American lantzman, an AEPi at the University of Georgia, with a long history of clandestine activities. Sammy Davis, Jr., would have been so proud.

So, raise your glass and shout "l'chaim" and a "groise nachas" to all of our new Jewish nominees, and hopefully convince them that the Iranian nuclear agreement, a/k/a the JCPOA, should be extinguished. If the same idea can be applied to the perfidious Marxist Squad and their anti-Semitic, anti-

Ron Ruthfield

Israel fellow travelers, there would be such a sense of genuine happiness in America and Israel.

Ron Ruthfield

BIDEN FAMILY, PUTIN TO OPEN NEW WHITE HOUSE RESORT ON BLACK SEA

In a move that has 20th century mobsters Meyer Lansky, Bugsy Siegel, and Lucky Luciano rolling the dice in their graves, Hunter Biden today announced from his art studio in a corner of the Oval Office that Wall Street bankers, high-stakes Las Vegas gamblers, and The Big Guy are partnering with Russia's strongman Vladmir Putin to build a Black Sea resort called Gulaggio. (**Pay attention. There are no corners in an oval-shaped office.**)

Biden's spokesman said the resort will include three different gulags, each with its own casino, restaurants, and rock pit, and that 100% of the guest rooms will be built for the handicapped according to standards established by the nation of Syria.

Ron Ruthfield

"The beachfront site will be very close to Odessa, a tiny village of more than 1 million residents, unexploded bombs, mine fields, dead Crimeans, and a paltry 337 miles from Chernobyl where day tours will be available for those who really want a radiant, scintillating adventure tour. In addition, tourists who would like to participate in the ongoing conflict between Russia and Ukraine (you can pick your side), military-grade weapons, including AK-47s and slingshots are available at no additional cost.

Despite the United States giving the Volodymyr Zelenskyy regime in Ukraine enough money to house, clothe, feed and arm every person in the Milky Way until the end of never, Hunter Biden's spokesman said the main Gulaggio nightclub called Sharansky's Showcase will also feature the Ukrainian head of state as a stand-up comic, his job prior to entering political show business.

Asked by a coterie of journalists, including those who weren't rolling on the floor laughing until their ribs hurt, about his son's new international venture, President Joe Biden leaned into his microphone and whispered, "I've NEVER shpokin' about my son's bidness dealings with him, you dirty sons-a-bitchees. EVER. Not even about my share of the p-p-p-profits."

As part of the deal, Russian officials have promised to release American prisoner Brittney Griner from a high-security penal colony where she's being held since she was caught drinking Red Bull mixed with cannabis oil and crushed birth control pills, and smuggling feminine products found by Russian police encased in a flattened basketball, similar to Griner's ego. Whether she'll be released to play in the WNBA again remains a three-point question.

Ron Ruthfield

"There's a chance Ms. Griner (she, her, perp, hustler) will be eligible for our work release program," a Russian official stated, adding that she can mix Black Russians and White Russians at one of our Gulaggio cocktail lounges. And at more than 203 centimeters tall with hands as large as jumbo frisbees, she will be able to handle a minimum of 12 food platters at one time, including what we think will become the specialty of the house: Pasta Puttanesca.

In other political news this week, John Fetterman (a/k/a Pennsylvania's Quasimodo) won a U.S. Senate seat by defeating The Wizard by a neck.

Ron Ruthfield

INTERNATIONAL CRIMINAL COURT CHARGES HAMAS WITH USING INCORRECT PRONOUNS

In what some military and political observers call a verbal "nakba" (Arabic for "Let's kill and torture everyone except us") the International Criminal Court (ICC), a well-known and open supporter of Israel and Jews currently in cemeteries, has indicted nine leaders of Hamas, including former New York City Mayor Bill de Blasio, for improper pronoun usage which carries a stiff, maximum penalty of six months of forced reading of the Oxford English Dictionary.

The indictment marks the first time in human and inhuman history that an assemblage of semi-friendly terrorists (I'm referring here to the United Nations and Hamas) has been targeted by global intelligence agencies and librarians.

Ron Ruthfield

A mass surveillance plan by Interpol, MI6, and the Mossad was conducted under the leadership of one of my former English professors, considered a leading expert of well-known words, syllables, and syntax, as opposed to sin tax, and someone who understands and personally implements the current 26,412 mandatory pronouns currently in use by socialists and trust-funded suburban hens.

"The investigation, which began earlier this year, took place in the Gaza Strip and in Muslim strip clubs in France, Germany, Italy, and England. Our operatives also worked hard to overhear conversations in Arabic at the U.S. southern border," commented Sir James Wokealot, head of Great Britain's crack MI6 intelligence unit which I swear has nothing to do with Hunter Biden.

So far, according to Wokealot, the snickering Hamas would-be martyrs and their heroic leaders who got used to their living in luxurious rental caves in Afghanistan have been arrested mainly for confusing he, she, them, em, zer, poseur, mountebank, pecksniffian, swami-like grifter, moonbat, Pelosian-like, among others.

Official documents, including audio and video evidence of the conversations among 1.2 million members of Hamas, including Black Lives Matter, Antifa, the Proud Boys, and Kanye West, were turned over to the International Court of Justice (ICJ) in The Hague, Netherlands, just last month.

According to its Wikipedia entry, the ICJ is the first and only permanent international court with jurisdiction to prosecute individuals for the international crimes of genocide, crimes against humanity, war crimes, the crime of aggression, and the misuse of English pronouns. The ICJ is distinct from the International Criminal Court, which is an instrument, once played by a church organist, of the United Nations that hears disputes between states, like California and Nevada or California and Utah or California and Oregon, the latter of which is moving all of its citizens to Beirut, Lebanon.

The trial of the nine indicted pronoun conspirators will begin immediately after tulip season.

Rashida Tlaib (D-Gaza City), one of a handful of Muslim U.S. Congresspersons and the only member of the House of Representatives who lives in a luxury condo in the Gaza Strip and a Winnebago in Michigan, made her position clear, saying, "My position is clear."

As part of her extracurricular windbaggery, she added, "I hate Israel but I love every pronoun even if it's an adjective."

President Biden, who has a long and reputable record of political chicanery is expected to be a witness at the trial, given his keen propensity to articulate and state his position as clear as a foggy day in London Town.

Will someone please call Scotland Yard and have Mr. Biden arrested the next time he's in Piccadilly Square for impersonating his likeness in Madame Tussaud's House of Wax?

NO HANUKKAH GIFTS THIS YEAR

We're only a couple of nights away from Hanukkah and I'm already spinning like a whirling dervish at more RPMs than a dreidel dripping from dipping it in potato latke oil, mostly on the side with the *gimel* (just ask any salesperson at your closest Walmart toy department and he/she will explain the *gimel, nun, shin, and hei.*)

To think that another eight days of the miracle of the Maccabees slapping the feta cheese out of the Greeks some 2,200 years ago and rededicating the Temple in Jerusalem makes me want to munch on some grape leaves, eggplant, black olives, and Zabar's creamed herring for at least eight nights or as long as the olive oil lasts for the pita bread. What few people realize is that the specific Jerusalem synagogue takeover was a bigger and better victory than when Smokin' Joe Frazier beat Muhammad Ali in the "Fight of the Century" in 1971.

But this year is different. Forget the gifts for the kids. No *gelt*, either. And don't get the idea that I'm the Hanukkah

Ron Ruthfield

Grinch. Waiting for Christmas to call me a "Grinch" will have more impact so be sober about your decision of when it would be most appropriate to smack me with another unbefitting appellation.

Actually, a more fitting sobriquet would be a Jewish Covidian, meaning a "frightened Hebrew humanoid caused by petulant, psychotic politicians and dissident Maoist newscasters bellowing about a cosmic, androgynous virus which will either eat someone over 65 or pass them by after spotting a more compelling target."

And because I'm beyond three-score and five years and a demonstrably juicier bullseye, if you believe I'm going out shopping for gifts for my nieces and nephews or some young'un who resembles Oliver Twist then I might suggest that you pour yourself a stiff alcoholic beverage with an olive and a twist. With a mask on.

Certainly, I could hire a personal shopper and take the chores off my hands. However, I don't believe that would work considering there are no personal shoppers within 75 miles of the North Carolina High Country, although we do have a Publix Super Market where shopping is a pleasure according to its corporate tagline. Besides, who sends a personal shopper to select haute couture merchandise next door to our finest retail outlet, the Dollar Tree where cashiers never bother to slip on a COVID mask unless they're robbing the bank in the same strip shopping center?

Please take note that I'm really philanthropic and one of the most decent guys I know on a personal basis. But I'm also totally aware that my young relatives must avoid Greeks bearing gifts, a certain signal that Judah Maccabee kept in his

Ron Ruthfield

frontal lobe as he took on and whipped King Antiochus of Epiphanes, thereby saving the Jewish People from certain extinction. That thought hasn't escaped me since I, too, may be rendered extinguished by those who will be waiting by the living room window peering out and waiting for the mail carrier to deliver Hanukkah packages to the usual suspects.

Come to think of it, there's always Amazon, a virtual store where I can always feel guilty about handing over my credit card number to a globalist. On second thought, I'm cutting this message short, putting on one of my four-layer cotton masks that I have in green, blue, and white, and driving 3 ½ hours to the closest Judaica shop to buy a new menorah and a multi-colored shammash just in time for Christmas (am I allowed to say "Christmas" anymore?).

Don't worry, kids. Next year we'll celebrate Hannukah with the whole family if the political class says we can once again be in the same room.

Ron Ruthfield

HOUSE DEMOCRATS OFFER NEW INITIATIVES AFTER CLAIMING VICTORY IN AFGHANISTAN

After a lightning-speed triumph over the Taliban in Afghanistan by the U.S. military, House Speaker Nancy Pelosi has announced some additional amendments to the proposed infrastructure bill now making its way through Congress.

While President Joe Biden and the First Lady were at Camp David (named after David Letterman, David Berkowitz a/k/a the Son of Sam serial killer, and King David) watching porno videos of their son Hunter on his recently lost but eventually discovered and recovered 20th Apple laptop, Pelosi offered the new proposals on Sunday, August 15, 2021, from her residence in a Section 8 housing compound in San Francisco.

Ron Ruthfield

"As Democrats and progressives now in control of the House of Representatives, we are calling for additional monies to be attached to the Gazillion-dollar (Editor's Note: that's 22 zeroes), 2,702-page legislation. An additional Quadrillion dollars (Editor's Note: that's 18 zeroes) is being earmarked to teach Pashto, Dari and Urdu as mandatory languages in all federally, state and local school systems."

"Because our nation is now saving Bazillions (Editor's Note: that's 24 zeroes) of dollars as a result of our rapid victory over the Taliban we will finally be able to provide our own American citizens and 40 million (Editor's Note: that's seven zeroes) illegal aliens with parsley and grits at every meal."

From his office in Havana, Secretary of Education Miguel Cardona added, "English in all schools will be an elective. However, Critical Race Theory and the Black Lives Matter manifesto will be mandated for students in public and private schools, K-12. Free Che Guevara T-shirts and berets will be available for all non-White students."

A spokesperson for the Department of Homeland Security said a few of the approximately 20,000 Afghan interpreters who helped the U.S. military and intelligence services during the almost 28 days of fighting, will be sent to St. Louis and Ferguson, MO, as well as Baltimore to help train their police departments on how to wear baggy pants and an authentic, handmade pakol hat or for a more casual look, a lungee turban.

Although women still will be forced to wear full body burkas with choices of black and blue (the black ones make it easier to cover up the black-and-blue marks) and get stoned to death for sleeping with a camel, according to a joint U.S.-Taliban announcement, they will be allowed to work in the

Ron Ruthfield

poppy fields thereby providing economic stability for their nation.

"The swift victory by our troops show the high level of our intelligence services and a reflection of the genius of our administration," said Jen Psaki, former White House Press Secretary. "We're all looking forward to putting 9/11 behind us."

MLB NAMES HUNTER BIDEN BATBOY, BAGMAN FOR AMERICAN LEAGUE ALL-STAR TEAM

It is now official.

Rumors had been swirling throughout America except for North Dakota whose entire population of 42 residents has recently moved to South Dakota, that President Biden's son, Hunter, had been on the short list to be the batboy for Major League Baseball's American League team, despite the outcry from thousands of baseball devotees who have demanded gender equality and have threatened to run onto the eponymous Coors Field drinking sudsy brew totally naked, sans towels, at the July 13, 2021, MLB All-Star Game which has been relocated from Atlanta to Denver because Coca-Cola, Delta Airlines, and a host of other America-First corporations decided to invoke their righteous indignation that the new Georgia voting rights law passed by the legislature, with Jim

Ron Ruthfield

Crow himself sliding into home plate, did not select a member of the LGBTQIA+ community to pass out and collect the Louisville Sluggers or clean up empty Coca-Cola containers in the dugout, and I swear I'm not making up any of this except for maybe seven or eight lines, and I'm not talking about lines of coke or a line-up of hookers having a three-bagger with Biden, or as Yogi Berra once said, "Pair up in threes and make sure it's with a narcissistic crack head sucking up gorgonzola cheese and lint from a shag carpet through two metal mini-straws, one inserted into each of his two nostrils," adding, "Even Napoleon had his Watergate."

The MLB spokesperson said he has given explicit instructions to Hunter Biden to stay clear of the pitcher's mound where the rosin bag can easily be mistaken for…well, you know, a satchel of snow or a bag of blow.

"But why Hunter?" asked one of the uninvited sports journalists from FOX News during the announcement. "Why should the president's progeny, a wealthy white dude, get to be bat boy when bat girl Rosie O'Donnell was available?"

"Apparently, you're not aware that Hunter Biden has a rich history of baseball in his personal and professional life," responded the spokesperson as he threw a fastball at the head of the FOX news reporter. "During his five years as a $50,000-a-month consultant, board member and bag man, including '20% for the Big Guy', of the Ukrainian energy firm, Burisma, Biden was also part of the starting line-up for the Kiev Cossacks where he was known as "Hunter the Bunter" and a "One-Hit-Wonder" and where his brief pitching career, according to video and scouting reports obtained by Major League Baseball, included a 0-45 win/loss record in three seasons, not only winning him an all-expense-paid trip to Monte Carlo but also

Ron Ruthfield

to a computer repair shop in Wilmington, DE, where his Apple Laptop has come under close scrutiny by his 18-month-old out-of-wedlock daughter, whose mommy is not only an active church member but a pole-dancing stripper whose savant offspring replaced an exclusive and technologically advanced FBI squad heading the investigation of what was on the computer.

In very clear, precise terms, Hunter has denied bringing the laptop to the shop although he also determined he was in a drug-induced haze and could have brought it in for repair to a crack house in Las Vegas or maybe it was stolen and someone else brought it in or perhaps the computer was actually a broken boom box that had collapsed or he could have taken it to a certified Apple repair shop in the Machu Picchu where there are no more residents.

Commissioner of Baseball Robert D. Manfred, Jr., also disclosed that the non-political MLB has named Nancy Pelosi as the home plate umpire while Chuck Schumer, Gerald Nadler, and Sheila Jackson Lee will man – whoops! – will be responsible for enforcing on-field rules and render decisions on calls such as whether baseball is nothing more than another field of dreams.

Ron Ruthfield

HURRY UP – I'M RUNNING OUT OF FINGERS

And then there were eight.

Every day it appears as though there will be no denouement to the spectacle taking place in Albany, New York, not Georgia. My personal and physical problem is that I have exactly two digits – my pinkie fingers – to count on before I begrudgingly bend over and yank my toes to help me keep track of the non-capital crimes in the capital city of New York.

Apparently, Gov. Andrew Cuomo (D-NY) has now been accused of fracturing the official Codes of Conduct of the Westminster and the American Kennel Clubs by suggesting to his former aide that he'd like to – her words, not mine – "mount her like a dog." According to the canine organization, the dilemma is whether he meant a Great Dane, Italian Greyhound, or a miniature Chihuahua although a spot check would have disclosed the good governor meant Dalmatian.

Ron Ruthfield

"We also accuse the governor of misappropriation of national canine monikers and places of origin," the spokesperson barked.

The aide, Lindsey Boylan, who currently is running for Manhattan Borough President, is the first of eight different females who have issued formal complaints about Cuomo's "sexual harassment and bullying" which has virtually nothing to do with Boston, English, or French Bulldogs, horned cattle, or toreadors.

One of his non-victim victims, another female assistant, claimed that the governor made her feel as though she was reliving her recent trip to Scotland. "While I was in his office, he stood up from behind his desk, put his arms around me, and pulled me close to his body," she remarked. "There's no question he had a tilt in his kilt," adding, "He was breathing so hard he could have been playing the bagpipes with the Albany chapter of the Royal Scots Dragoon Guards."

The "mounting" allegations have prompted forceful calls by everyone for Cuomo to resign or at least promise to step down right after the 45th woman lodges a complaint despite an investigation by New York Attorney General Letitia James and a New York State Assembly–led impeachment inquiry.

According to a poll by Pew Research, at least 850 million American citizens have registered their dislike for Cuomo's narcissistic and misogynistic behavior and have called for his termination or resignation, although Columbia University, New York University, and Fordham University have already offered the governor tenured professorships in Criminology and Government Ethics. The 850 million, it was noted, included Democrats, Republicans, Libertarians, communists,

Ron Ruthfield

socialists, Fascists, Black Lives Matter members, Red Coats, administrators of the 1619 Project, the North American Man/Boy Love Association, the Lincoln Project, and Antifa.

"Resign?" Cuomo asked with just a touch of gasconade and defiance. "I'm getting tired of this cancel culture! They actually want me to leave my office? No sirree, not until I finish my job of placing more COVID victims into nursing homes."

Ron Ruthfield

I AM A HERO

I never thought it would get this bad. Especially in our small, uber-friendly town of Boone lodged in a valley among the lush cerulean mountains of the Blue Ridge set into the Appalachian Range in North Carolina some 15 minutes northwest of the Continental Divide. (Good thing no one ever fell into that divide; the big crack would have killed 'em.)

As a volunteer auxiliary police officer, I was called into action four days ago when a ruckus broke out at 2 AM. Darn, the major scuffle was right near the middle of town, according to the voice on the short-wave police radio band that I typically listen to on a round-the-clock basis. Heck, wouldn't you in these times of insurrection wanna tune into trouble? I've always felt I had a duty and responsibility to protect life, limb and property of my fellow citizens, except communists.

"Throw caution to the wind," I said to myself, as I hopped into my 2002 Dodge Ram-Tough pick-up (red with white pinstripes) and blazed a trail to King St. just short of the speed

Ron Ruthfield

of light and fright. King St., it just so happens, is the hub of activity in our community, except for the more upscale Walmart and Dollar Stores snuggled gently among asphalt-paved parking lots between three of our better restaurants, Applebee's, Chili's and Hungry Howie's. "Caution should only be used on traffic lights," I whispered in my own ear. "This town is in crisis and needs me now."

As I passed the CITGO station and convenience store (a really good place to stock up on cheap cigarettes, Monster beverages, and a variety of jerky) I noticed right there on the left – or on the left without the "right there" – a man who seemed to be oppressed by the establishment. I could tell because he had a sign in one handheld high declaring, "I'm being oppressed by the establishment." Good thing I was able to read that cardboard message in the flickering, dusty light filled with swarming mayflies.

And the nerve of that well-dressed church-goin' woman who was right there on the left with that man swinging her navy patent-leather purse at his head simply because he had a knife in his right hand and the sign in his left – well, I'll tell ya right now that she was at fault. A definite part of the societal problem of white privilege without a shred of guilt. She knew full well she wasn't supposed to be carrying the color navy in the summer months, anyway!

Jumping into action, I threw that lady to the ground despite her kickin' and hollerin' at me like a wounded bobcat then threw the plastic cuffs around her wrists which were now behind her back. I admonished and warned her, "If you move, I'm gonna taze ya." My training kicked in as I began to do my breathing and visualization exercises to maintain my self-possessed equanimity.

Ron Ruthfield

And just at the moment I thought I had the situation under control, oh Lord, that young white man with the sign? He busted the wooden stake holding the stapled cardboard over my head while screaming, "I hate cops, even if they're old, balding auxiliary cops!" Although I didn't hear everything quite clearly, he said something about my failure to recognize systemic racism and white oppression.

Blood everywhere and don't even mention the headache. Lasted for three days. Much of it is now a blur, although my broken leg should heal in less than six months. At least that's what the surgeon said. Oh, and the pain in my four broken ribs will feel a whole lot better in a few weeks.

But know that I'm not giving up. No, sirree. Nobody said this would be easy, but neither did anyone tell me when I dashed to the melee that I'd wind up in the ICU. However, that's not the point. We're creating a better world in which police and their auxiliaries, the really bad guys, no longer exist.

However, once I'm off suspension and probation for failure to recognize systemic oppression, I'll be back making Boone safe once again. I've decided not to throw in my baton just yet.

Even if it kills me.

Ron Ruthfield

AMERICA'S NUCLEAR DEAL WITH IRAN PASSES GAS

Covert sources close to the negotiations between the United States and Iran have leaked vital information to your friendly correspondent (who, as you know, has never once made a reportorial error) including that American negotiators have reached a final agreement with Iran via a new Joint Comprehensive Plan of Action (JCPOA), also known as the SAID (Screw America and Israel Doctrine).

The most important component of the deal, according to documents accidentally smuggled out of the negotiations by a Klezmer accordion player in the creases of his instrument, is that the Iranians will supply every American citizen with a lifetime supply of Ayatollah Cola, the most popular domestic carbonated beverage in Iran, Venezuela, and Cuba. According to Anthony Blinken, U.S. Secretary of State, the soda pop, introduced in the 1979 Iranian Revolution upon the return to Tehran from France by Ayatollah Khomeini, uses natural gas

Ron Ruthfield

primarily from goats, and is domestically bottled by prisoners and child labor in a number of Iranian cities, including Beverly Hills.

The smuggled notes also quoted the founding head of Iran's Islamic Revolutionary Guards, Al-Killya Khameini who said, "We'd love to teach the world to sing in perfect harmony."

By a wink, a Blinken, and a nod, the accords were finally pushed through with those at the negotiating table making a toast by drinking a mixture of Ayatollah Cola and Kool-Aid.

"The final wording of the document has yet to be completed but there are definitive swaps between both nations that are historic and at the same time will bring peace to the Middle East and beyond, except for the 112 ship containers filled with nuclear warheads. Iran will be permitted to produce additional nukes no later than the U.S. Presidential elections a year from November. At that point, Donald Trump will be in a federal lock-up on charges of acrimonious cage fighting with former presidential candidate and Secretary of State Felonia Clintonia von Pantsuit."

"Bargaining was extremely tough," according to the source. "But we eventually convinced the Iranian mullahs that we will deed all property in Crown Heights and Williamsburg in Brooklyn and 74% of Boca Raton in exchange for the hydrogen bombs in the ship containers," the operative said. In addition, we have made an official commitment that we will compel the Israeli government by military force, if necessary, to give up all of Israel, including Miami Beach, and expel all Jews, Christians, and Voodoo adherents. That idea was floated some years ago by back-channel negotiators, including former U.S.

Ron Ruthfield

President Barack Hussein Obama who, while on an official visit, once tried posing as a native-born Israeli to gain entry to a Jews-only gay nightclub in Tel Aviv.

The as-yet unsigned document also includes a major clause that stops all terror funding by Iran except for funds earmarked for Hamas, Hezbollah, Palestinian Islamic Jihad, Al Qaeda, The Southern Poverty Law Center (now an affiliate of The Taliban), and the American Federation of Teachers, although the head of the union, Randi Weingarten will receive a 200% salary increase. Readers might recall that Weingarten, an open and out-of-the-closet, self-avowed lesbian, was the very same female who President William Jefferson Clinton claimed, "I did not have sex with that woman."

Iran's demands include that the Islamic theocracy be the key sponsor of Tel Aviv's Gay Pride Parade, although the LGBTQIA+ in Israel has made it clear that a maximum of only 250 Israeli citizens can be hanged from construction cranes in public during Gay Pride Month.

One of the unnamed stoolies whispered that the talks were so tense and tentative that several of the meditators thought the negotiations were like driving into a cemetery and the GPS said, "You have reached your final destination."

The only potential stumbling block is that President Joe Biden must sign the final doctrine while attempting to walk up the portable airplane stairs leading to Air Force One no later than his fourth tumble even if the steps are laden with sandbags.

Even if the Commander-in-Chief runs out of gas.

Ron Ruthfield

THE JEWISH-MUSLIM RACE TOWARD PEACE

As much of the world knows by now, Israel and several of the Arab countries in the Middle East and Muslim-majority African nations are going through a renaissance, an almost romantic revival of sorts that promises to bring a much more peaceful and stable world.

Naturally, Speaker of the U.S. House Nancy Pelosi has called the upcoming peace accords between the Jewish State and their new Arab partners "a distraction", a statement which I, for one, totally forgive since she uttered that piece of brilliant news smack-dab in the middle of her AA meeting after drinking a half-gallon of cheap gin mixed with Yoo-Hoo, no ice.

On a personal note, I can foretell the future when Emiratis from the UAE, citizens of Bahrain and Oman, Chadians, Malawians, and other people of good will actually create personal friendships with every-day Israelis. In fact, my

Ron Ruthfield

background as a world-renowned diplomat for the United States has allowed me to have access to some of the most polished, savvy and respected emissaries from many of the nations that will be quickly signing peace agreements with the Jewish State.

As a result of my close association with key cultural and political figures in Israel, I've been given permission to host many of those new visitors at the Western Wall where I've already established a cadre of cohorts who will invite these visitors to Shabbat dinners at their homes. Strictly kosher, of course.

The strategy is to accommodate vast numbers of visitors from those newly established relationships via a person-to-person effort, making it much smoother for a full transition to peace. Once the program is in effect, here's how it's probably going to flow at the wall:

"Ahmed, I want you to meet Shloymie and his wife, Leah. They're the Aaronsons and are originally from Chicago."

"Nice to meet you, Shloymie and Leah. You have children?"

"Why shouldn't we have children?" asks Leah who, like every Jewish woman on Planet Earth, always answers a question with a question. It's also in a tone that without a doubt makes her authentically Jewish. "We have nine. Eight daughters and a son. The girls can't find husbands in Israel because the men are too independent. You know any nice Jewish boys from Abu Dhabi?"

Ron Ruthfield

"Not really, but I'll look for a few when I return home. How 'bout a few secular Muslims? Today, you can't tell the difference."

"That would be a shanda, Ahmed! We'd have to sit shiva if anything came of it," Leah responded.

"Before we go home for Shabbos dinner, you wanna lay some tefillin?" asks Shloymie.

"No thank you, Shloymie," says Ahmed, not really knowing that wrapping leather straps around his left arm and fingers might stop the flow of blood circulating through his entire body. Plus, he would have no idea why he's putting a box on his head.

They all walk to the Aaronson's modest apartment where seven of the daughters are waiting to begin the Sabbath dinner. The eighth daughter, they tell Ahmed, lives in a Kibbutz near the Gaza border, and their son is in the IDF's Givati brigade serving at a base also close to the Gaza Strip.

"Oy, vey," says Ahmed as he slaps his right hand on his forehead. "Inshallah, I hope he comes home safely. You've already had enough tsouris."

After a few baruchas and enough Yarden Cabernet Sauvignon to go around, everyone takes their seat at the table.

"How 'bout a slice of that challah," asks Ahmed. "I understand it goes well with chopped liver and schmaltz."

Without the slightest pause, the oldest of the daughters at home, Sarah, slices a chunk of the braided bread and hands it to Ahmed. "Now this is a real mechiah," he says. "Can you give me the recipe, Leah?"

Ron Ruthfield

"Why shouldn't I give you the recipe?" asks Leah.

As the evening wears on and it's time for Ahmed to go back to his hotel, he can only think of how much of a beautiful future his countrymen will have with Israel.

He hails an Arab-driven taxi, relaxes in the back seat, and says to the driver, "If the Democrats win the upcoming election in the United States, I hope, they, too, will make peace with Israel.

"Now that would be a real miracle."

Ron Ruthfield

AMERICA THE BEAUTIFUL AND SOMEWHAT UGLY

This is what America now means to me.

It's the middle of September 2020 and my brain is still sizzling by seven months of suspense over the Dr. Anthony Fauci Wuhan, Chinese, COVID-19, Toyota Corona Wet Market, Dry Market, Moist Market, Super Market, 2019-nCoV Acute Respiratory Disease, SARS-2, Non-Kosher Seafood Market, Pneumonia, Novel Coronavirus Pneumonia, Severe Pneumonia with Novel Pathogens Pandemic.

Don't even mention the November presidential elections.

If you were not aware of it, while we've been secreted in our germ-free homes all of us are now wholly owned by subsidiaries of the U.S. Government, Amazon, and our local supermarket, which is probably owned and operated by Amazon.

Ron Ruthfield

Schools are open or closed depending on the whims of a group of psychotics, including some Democrat Marxists, Bolsheviks, chiropractors, and community organizers.

Zombies meander through lines at stores' registers with tape measures and yardsticks to make certain they're six feet away from other zombies measuring devices. Masks made from every kind of material (I saw a man today wearing one made from Saran Wrap) are more common than veils at a belly-dancing contest in Egypt. One would hope you're following the strict rules handed down by lunatics. Like watching football and baseball games on television with cardboard fans in the seats, and pre-recorded cheering and booing by riveted adherents. And if you're prone to learning the lyrics and music to the New Black Lives Matter Anthem, be sure to tune in with the sound on. Remember, Marxism matters. It's a beautiful sight when the BLM renditions are played before The Star-Spangled Banner, the copyright of which is most likely owned by Amazon, with the waving of the American flag – uh, wait, no American flags allowed.

And hey, while you're at it, why not take a knee next to your sofa in your living or game room, preferably not in the groin.

Remember, this might be the only time in your life when you will live through the merriment of total societal collapse, an event not experienced by many since those of us who lived through the French Revolution or when Rasputin bit a trio of bullets on a snowy December night at the Palace of the Yusupovs on the Moika River in St. Petersburg just outside of Tampa, FL, although some historians dispute Rasputin's actual location of his death. In fact, some continue to believe he's still

Ron Ruthfield

alive and is the grandfather of Vladimir Putin who shortened his name by removing the Ras.

Knowing that we might have to live in re-education camps for a while, start packing like you were going to summer camp. And for goodness sakes, don't forget to write your name with a Magic Marker on the elastic band of your underwear.

Meantime, it's probably an excellent idea to spend the next several months visiting every national park in the country loaded up with beer, Vodka, and 10-times refillable prescriptions for Valium and OxyContin. In the event your doctor won't give you the prescription, I have several contacts with Antifa leaders who, for a small fee, will be happy to provide your highness with some alternative therapies. Better to do that than be cancelled or fired from your job for not being woke enough.

With all of that said, I cannot wait until our official flu season begins, signaling that we all might be back to normal by the end of the year, although I cannot be certain which year that might be.

Ron Ruthfield

SARA THREATENS TO PUT BIBI ON HUNGER STRIKE AFTER MISSING CALL FROM PRESIDENT BIDEN

In an apparent misstep in communications between the White House and the office of Israel's Prime Minister Benjamin Netanyahu, it has been revealed that President Biden's long-awaited call to the leader of the Jewish state went awry.

Official sources in Israel claimed that the much-anticipated call from POTUS never went through proper communications channels and somehow the telephone at the prime minister's office got crossed with his home line. The unnamed source said the call was initiated January 21, the day after President Biden's inauguration.

Ron Ruthfield

A Shin Bet agent on duty in the residence of the prime minister has acknowledged there were some awkward moments as a result of the mix-up, including a terse, tense conversation between Netanyahu and his wife, Sara.

"It's about time you're home! I've been looking for you for hours. And don't tell me I'm kvetching. I even tried calling you at the office and they told me you were in three different meetings. Where were you? Couldn't you even pick up the phone and let me know you'd be a half-hour late? You think you're some kind of a Mad Men star? I had something so important to tell you! Now you're going to have to wait until after you eat dinner. I'm telling you gornisht. Why do you always do this to me?"

"I don't ALWAYS do this to you. Most of the time I'm in meetings. Come on, it's important, you said. Tell me NOW, not after I eat my falafel wrap and kneidlach soup."

"Okay. Yossi called."

"Yossi who?"

"Yossi Biden, that's WHO!"

"So, what did he say?"

"He said he meant to call you a couple of days ago but lost your office number. He wanted to speak to me anyway so he could apologize for calling me Sadie the last time we spoke. But this time he called me Stormy. What's with him?"

"Stormy? As in Stormy Daniels? Maybe he thinks he's Bill Clinton at a Girl Scout convention. Besides, I must have given Yossi my private number at least a dozen times. I'm not sure if

Ron Ruthfield

he knows where ANYTHING is and can't even remember names."

"Never mind what Yossi remembers. Sit down and eat. You'll call him back tomorrow right after I send him a huge box of one of the 10 plagues in Jewish history."

"Which one?"

"Stale bagels."

Ron Ruthfield

AGAIN, IT'S THE JEWS BY A NOSE!

There they go again! Now try and convince me that Jews don't control the banks; the military-industrial complex; the global food supply; every major oil company drilling in Saudi Arabia, Venezuela and downtown Detroit; all major league professional teams in cricket, rugby, archery, bowling, football (both kinds), baseball, basketball, hockey, badminton, ping pong, pickleball, and midget tossing.

Everyone in the United States – trust me on this one – knows they collect the money from toll booths on interstate highways in North America, including the Yukon Territories and Haiti. And let's not forget that Israel has the concession for tent rentals at the annual Hajj in Mecca and has first rights to the charity collection boxes at St. Peter's Basilica in Vatican City.

Now, they're even attempting to seize control of the Jewdiciary in what they call the "Jewish Homeland" called Israel or what some notable and popular personalities and

Ron Ruthfield

intellectuals in other economically developed countries, including Mauritania and the Maldives, call the Little Satan, meaning Israel.

"Jewdicial reform?" asked U.S. President Joe Biden in a moment of candor while eating the face off of a toddler being held in her father's arms during a TV presser. "I think not," he continued. "Real reform will be obvious when we finalize our renewed nuclear with Iran. Or is it Iraq? Iceland? Well, I know it begins with an I. Ireland? No?

"Did I mention I never discussed – not even twice – anything with my son, Hunter, about his business dealings, other than one time that he advised me to open an offshore bank account. Certainly not his relationships with companies in the Ukraine or China, which are both controlled by the Jews" the Commander-in-Chief remarked while fondling the breasts of the closest female who turned out to be his Press Secretary, Karine Jean-Pierre who seemed to enjoy it despite her proclivity, according to casual observers and her wife, toward an alternative lifestyle.

I mean for goodness sake! It has now become a neoteric exercise for some of the most cerebral and high-profile savants like America's very own Rep. Pramila Jayapal (D-WA), head of the Congressional Progressive Party-Until-Morning Caucus.

At a recent anti-Israel celebration while carrying a 20-foot by 30-foot Palestinian flag, Jaya-my-pal bellowed, "Israel is a racist and apartheid state! I should know. I used to be a Jewess long before I became anti-Semitic. In fact, I found out some years ago that every one of my male ancestors was named Bernie, dating back to Neanderthal Man which is why I

Ron Ruthfield

endorsed Sen. Bernie Sanders (KOOK-VT) in the last presidential election."

Jayapal added she's now a lay leader of The First Church That's Sending Me To Hell, headquartered in a janitorial closet in the Watergate Hotel in Washington, D.C. Word has it that another 26 Democrat Marxists have affiliated themselves with the church, including former Sen. George McGovern's (D-SD) corpse.

And talking about Jews by a nose and a longshot, it is certainly not by a longshot but an entire series of shots that kept COVID-19 away from the Chosen People. Just do a modicum of research about the vaccine and you'll definitely come across the name of Albert Bourla, a triple-nostril and conspiratorial Jew who as Chief Executive Officer of the international drug manufacturer Pfizer spearheaded and sniffed out a remedy for the deadly virus, which unfortunately, wasn't discovered in time to revive Sen. McGovern as a result of his being deceased eight years.

The most revelatory aspect of COVID is that not a single Hebrew – and there's a bunch of them – was infected. Google it if you're skeptical. It was stupefying to observe how many non-Jews lined up at synagogues around the globe, including the North Pole, to become inoculated and in the case of post-pubescent men, circumcised as well.

Robert F. Kennedy, Jr., a candidate for the presidency in the 2024 election, remarked, "Look, I'm not a Jew-hater like Grandpa Joe was, or even a Sinophobe, but how and who developed a deadly virus that doesn't affect Jews? To be specific, American, European and Chinese Jews? Simple luck? I think not."

Ron Ruthfield

An excellent and probative question, considering I am an Ashkenazi (the last four letters don't count) Jew – a White one – and never once did I experience a cough, a sneeze, pneumonia, or a yearning to eat wonton soup or attach myself to a ventilator, or any other COVID symptoms, including an outbreak of dandruff or unmanicured fingernails. And, as a dues-paying member of the Ashkenazi (I said the last four letters don't count!) Jewish-American Underground and Fun Club and its affiliated Chinese chapters, it came to my attention via a covert note in a kosher fortune cookie that 10 Hebrew tribes are now charging rental fees on 98% of the tents for the homeless in San Francisco, Los Angeles, and New York City.

Upon learning of the rental fees, the head of the Anti-Defamation League, Jonathan Greenbacks, demanded that his organization get a 20% cut to help support the Democrat Marxist Party and re-election for members of the Squad.

A big price to pay for self-hating Jews.

"LET'S MAKE A DEAL" LAUNCHED BETWEEN GENIUS COLLEGE GRADS AND U.S. TREASURY

After a tense couple of weeks of protracted and secretive negotiations, the leading organization in the United States for brilliant college and university graduates, a/k/a The Leading Organization in the United States for Brilliant College and University Graduates, have come to an agreement with Janet Yellen, Secretary of the Treasury, on the $10,000 and $20,000 rebates for student tuition.

Finally, the terms have been settled for approximately the same amount of funds – $170 trillion – which are the aggregate endowments of Harvard, Yale, Columbia, and Patrice Lumumba University in Moscow.

Unfortunately, the mortician for the now-deceased Monty Hall, one of the world's most outstanding financial mediators,

Ron Ruthfield

could not keep the TV game show host alive long enough for him to participate in the negotiations. Sadly, the Final Curtain was called on Mr. Hall about five years ago.

The somewhat combative discussions, according to both sides, finally concluded successfully with each of the parties signing off on the final deal in the office of Dr. Vivek Murthy, Surgeon General of the United States. President Biden endorsed the agreement with a giant "X" on the signature line, asking with great dignity, "Where's my bicycle? I wanna go home."

"The $10,000 per student rebate for conventional loans and the $20,000 credit for those who were given Pell Grants will be swapped with a rather unique quid pro quo formula," said Chancellor Spuds McTater from the University of Idaho at Coeur D'Alene speaking on behalf of the students and the National Center for White Nationalists.

Federal Pell Grants typically are awarded only to undergraduate students who display exceptional financial need. They do not have to have earned a bachelor's, graduate, or professional degree. Some of the recipients, said McTater, will receive the $20,000 as soon as they are released from incarceration from federal penitentiaries and state prisons for murder, rape, and other violent crimes.

Those who have earned degrees while behind bars will get bonuses of 50% but must have received a minimum of four tattoos while in custody: two on their faces and one on each arm measuring a total of 60 square inches. Repeat offenders will receive an additional $20,000 as soon as they are re-released.

"However," said Dr. Murthy, "as payback all students receiving the $10,000 and $20,000 tuition credits will have to forcibly forget the amount of information they learned while studying at a college or university. For instance, if someone became a cardiologist at one of our outstanding medical schools, he or she will have to forget how many ventricles the heart contains, thereby paying back some of the knowledge they may have picked up during their studies. Negating their familiarity with colonoscopies and catheter insertions would qualify as well.

"In the event a student who has received the funds decides to remember everything he or she was taught, then I'm afraid we'll have to operate on their hippocampuses (which have nothing to do with large animals on college and university property) located in the brain's temporal lobe which is where episodic memories are formed and indexed for later access," Dr. Murthy concluded.

One student from the University of Delaware said he wouldn't mind at all giving up his knowledge of quantum theory, geophysics, or fluid dynamics especially since he never took a course in any of those subjects anyway. "Just hand over the bucks and let me do what I wanted to do in the first place, which was to become a scuba-diving pizza delivery man or a train pushing Oshiya, who's the person in Japan who crams as many people onto a subway train as possible until the doors close with a mere 22 arms caught between the two doors of each car. Ironically, the latest report from the Japanese government is that during the past decade, a bare minimum of only 48,120 arms have been torn off as a result of a highly competent and sophisticated system that some transportation experts dub A Farewell To Arms.

Secretary Yellen also announced that she has given full authority for all members of Major Pronoun Groups who test

Ron Ruthfield

at an I.Q. level of more than 77 do qualify to simply take the money and run.

Ron Ruthfield

PRESIDENT 45 INDICTED FOR 45TH TIME

The Attorney General of Hawaii tonight announced the 45th indictment of former President Donald J. Trump, the 45th Commander-in-Chief of the United States, claiming there is definitive proof that the former head of state is responsible for the blazing inferno on the island of Maui that so far has caused more than 110 people to lose their lives.

The indictment follows on the footsteps of 44 other criminal charges slammed against the former president for a variety of alleged crimes, including a potentially illicit hot and steamy affair with the current junior senator from Hawaii, Maisy Hirono (D) who told an unidentified reporter (well, if you really want to know, it was the son of the late Hawaiian singer Don Ho, whose first name is Gung) from the Honolulu Star-Advertiser that Trump failed to pay her after agreeing to a verbal contract for an evening of pleasure.

According to the newspaper report, President Trump still owes Hirono the agreed upon price of $10 but a Trump

Ron Ruthfield

spokesperson headquartered in the Trump Waikiki Resort on Oahu, claimed that even a sawbuck wouldn't have been worth it based on his own previous experience with overweight, angry female politicians.

In addition, the newspaper claimed that island authorities had substantial evidence that President Trump had to be the one person who started the out-of-control fire and quoted the Lahaina Fire Chief, Kumon Iwana Leiya.

"We were able to retrieve a matchbook cover from the Trump Waikiki Resort in the wreckage of a cigar store located right next to a cancer clinic. Although we understand that Mr. Trump doesn't smoke, we are making every effort to search for fingerprints on the evidence which will undoubtedly show that Trump is the leading suspect for committing the widespread arson. Additionally, former Trump attorney, Michael Cohen, called our department and offered to serve as a witness at the former president's upcoming trial that Trump used to like to play with matches when he was four years old.

"Further, we recovered 12 scorched tiki torches from a Kapalua Resort luau that are virtually identical to the ones used in the Charlottesville Unite the Right rally in August 2017, a five-year span almost to the day. A coincidence? I think not! And we also believe an underlying reason for committing this heinous crime by Trump was to make himself look more orange."

Meanwhile, President Biden was asked to comment on the ferocious flames that engulfed a major portion of Maui.

"That fire was in Maui?" the president asked. "Geez, had I known that I would have sent thousands of bicycles for people to flee from the flames. Hey, you know I was in Maui once.

Ron Ruthfield

Isn't that the place where there's a huge hole on top of a mountain? Yeah, a few years ago I took my son Hunter, and we walked up the 10,000 feet from sea level in less than 20 minutes. I remember because Hunter was high (Hunter was always high) as a result of being at a high elevation. We landed on the pinnacle, hopped on our bicycles – hey, man, I'm not kidding about this – and rolled down that mountain in record time despite my tumbling off my J.C. Higgins' Mountain Bike from Sears-Roebuck seven times, each time on my head – and I wasn't even wearing a helmet!"

"Yes," said one of his aides. "Which proves once and for all that our president has the stamina and mental acuity to continue leading the country with his vast economic, military, executive, and foreign policy credentials, including his ability to speak English at the 6th grade level. His entire staff believes that will serve him well when he takes on the role as chief negotiator with Iran and securing a new Iranian comprehensive peace plan especially now that Robert Malley, formerly the administration's chief negotiator, was caught releasing national security information to our enemies."

The aide added that the president made certain that Malley, who also served in the Obama Administration and was responsible for negotiating the first JCPOA with Iran, got a professorship at Princeton University, thereby avoiding a long stretch at the United States Penitentiary at Leavenworth.

Biden and his entourage made the comments at Rehoboth Beach, DE, while Maui was burning, and the president was on his 45th vacation since taking office.

Ron Ruthfield

THE UNITED STATES' TOWER OF BABBLE

Once again, in its estimable conduct and aggressive, positive posture on behalf of free speech for every American, the Josef Bidenovich Administration has established its own Tower of Babble.

According to a spokeszombie for government apparatchik Aleksandr Mayorski, Minister of Homeland Securitat, Pravda, and Word Procurement, a Czarina of Disinformation, Misinformation, Bad Information, Awful Information, Ugly Information, Lack of Information, and No Information has been appointed.

"I feel honored to be able to allow every American citizen to say whatever, whenever and wherever they want," said Nina "Lolita" Jankowicz in her new position as head of the Disinformation Governance Board, adding "except those who like to speak freely."

Ron Ruthfield

"The new guidelines will apply to the entire population of the United States and its territories, except for Bhutan and government employees who take too many bathroom breaks. We will take those cases to trial as we flush them out.

"Of course, we will always attempt to politically balance exceptions and exemptions to the rule of 'Shut up or we'll bury you in Gorky Park' especially with specific justices on the Supreme Court. Note that Socialist, Collectivist, Marxist-chartered organizations, and academics in Ivy League Educational Indoctrination Institutions will not fall under the new governance guidelines, nor will Oberlin College and a number of similar institutions that display a "certain gravitas" toward Bolshevism and catalepsy.

"Neither will citizens on the government's Official Woke List or illegal aliens as prepared by the Board of Directors of Black Lives Matter, the Communist Party U.S.A., and Randi Weingarten, president of the American Federation of Teachers, Education Propagandists, and Frightfully Torpid Mental Cases."

Shortly after the announcement of the new department, this reporter overheard a telephone conversation – may lightning strike me on my lips if I'm fibbing about this – between Pytor Paranoiavich, a local block captain appointed by former President Barack Obama in St. Petersburg (Florida, not Russia) and Natasha Pelosky, a high-ranking Democrat whose political reputation almost equaled her ranking as the Person of the Decade for her widespread usage of daily Botox injections and hiding in beauty salons during COVID-19 breakouts.

Ron Ruthfield

"Comrade Pelosky," asked Praranoiavich during the 19-second conversation, "will individual thinking and suggestions be permitted once we've instituted all of the board's protocols?"

"Ha, ha, ha, ha, ha, ha, ha, nah, nah, nah, nah....." Pelosky snorted as the sound of paper being ripped was heard in the background on the speakerphone. Presumably, it was either former President Trump's State of the Union speech or the U.S. Constitution. Muffled applause from her fan base was audible.

Rumors began to swirl in both clockwise and counterclockwise directions after "Lolita" was appointed. One well-known authority on truth-telling, former President Bill Clinton, claimed George Orwell actually wrote in the 1940s that not only would a Chinese video concept called TikTok become a reality but that a Minister of Truth or Consequences would become a public figure and a city in New Mexico.

"Miss Information," as Jankowicz is now known, actually sang a parody sounding like a pack of wild coyotes while attempting to mimic Mary Poppins in a resurfaced TikTok video. "I want to be rich, famous, and powerful! Step on all my enemies and never do a thing," Jankowicz sang accompanied by a piano. "Who do I f__k to be famous and powerful? I've done everything I can and now the rest is up to you," she appeared to add, no doubt a résumé enhancer. Apparently, there were no volunteers, not even her husband.

Jankowicz also cumbrously attempted to discredit the story of Hunter Bidenovich's laptop that mysteriously landed in a Delaware computer repair store, and claimed the Steele dossier funded by the Hillary Clinton campaign was actually

Ron Ruthfield

the truth and the link between President Trump and actual Russian collusion funded by Republicans.

Not even Tom Clancy could have written this bizarre tale of indoctrination, perfidy, chaos, and leftist insanity. And Elon Musk with his $43 billion Twitter investment won't even come close to tweeting away these iconoclastic Huns.

Ron Ruthfield

A DECADE FROM NOW

The year is 2032.

A few of my longtime friends from Florida and North Carolina decided to journey to New York City for a guys' weekend. All of us knew some cultural and political refinements had occurred in The Big Apple, now known as The Big Red Apple, since it was peeled with a dull paring knife during the nationwide Socialist and Marxist riots a decade prior.

Never mind the COVID-19 pandemic at the same time; Marx took Manhattan, the Bronx and Staten Island, too.

And since none of us had been to the city since 2020, we were warned by online travel sites that addressing and speaking about certain subjects were unwelcome. Questions like, "Hey, where's the statue of Columbus?" were forbidden ever since the captain of the Santa Maria got hammered in his own circle by the Bolshevik Buccaneers, an organization that found its footings in the Central Park Lake.

Ron Ruthfield

Landing on a Thursday afternoon at what is now known as The de Blasio People's Airport (some people still call it La Guardia, which can result in a fine of 50 kopeks if you're overheard by airline personnel or maintenance workers), I waited at the lone vodka bar for the arrival of my three buddies.

"You pay the bourgeois price," I was told by a curt-but-well-dressed bartender whose wardrobe appeared to be similar to the ones donned by overweight, female East German railroad engineers in the 1960s.

"You have more than one price for the same drink?" I asked hesitatingly.

"Da," she shouted, embracing her new mother tongue as smoothly as the potato vodka slid down my throat as she clutched that same dull paring knife. "Proletariat and bourgeois. Politburo and Duma members drink free. We take cash or Russian Express credit cards."

"What about American Express credit cards?" I asked politely.

"Nyet," she barked like a Siberian Husky.

By the time I paid my bill with U.S. dollars and received a couple of rubles in change, my friends appeared. (I left the rubles as a tip, fearing that if I didn't my ration card would be shredded.)

I shrugged off the incident and, like my friends, looked forward to a marvelous, long weekend in the city. We picked up our luggage at the carousel, grabbed an Uber-mensch and headed to the Pushkin Plaza on 58th St., but not before we were mandated to go through three checkpoints – one at the airport, one on the Triboro Bridge, and the final one operated by a homeless person trying to wipe the car windows with a dirty rag at the first stoplight – established the previous decade to make certain we weren't spreading the Wu Flu.

A couple of hours later, the four of us met in the lobby and headed on foot to find a place to eat near the hotel. Walking a few blocks south, we stumbled on a place located in the Andropov Arcade along what is now the Molotov Mile. The flashing red lights against a black background caught our attention: BLM Diner.

We walked in and asked for a table for four.

"You're not permitted in this restaurant," bellowed the cisgender human. "Clearly, the four of you are not supporters of the BLM Movement so you'll have to leave. Perhaps you can find a place more suitable for your kind, like the Carnegie Deli!"

"Wait a minute," said one of my friends. "That deli has been closed for a dozen years! Are you canceling us? We thought BLM stood for bacon, lettuce, and mayonnaise which is why we came in."

We knew something wasn't kosher about the place, so we left.

Another block south, we spotted another eatery's signage spelling out in an oversize-font named The Borscht Belt and in a smaller font that read "Where You Can Eat It and Loosen It." Obviously, that was for us. A holdover from the days when brisket, pastrami, corned beef, a metal bowl filled with chopped liver, and an egg cream tasted like All Lives Mattered when it came to delicious dining.

Ron Ruthfield

After we left, something strange happened. Before we even got back to the hotel, all four of us decided we would each be on the next plane to our individual destinations we all called home.

We should have known better than to have visited New York City, especially when we discovered that the name Broadway was being changed for being too misogynistic, and that the Great White Way had turned off its lights.

Permanently.

Ron Ruthfield

SHOCKING: SURPRISE SPEAKER AT GLASGOW CLIMATE CONFERENCE DIVULGES PRESIDENTIAL SECRET

In what can only be described as an "earth-shaking" (which seismologists actually refer to by the very complex scientific term, earthquake) announcement, officials at the United Nations Climate Change Conference in Glasgow (also known as the 26th Conference of the Parties where attendees wore cone-shaped cardboard hats; blew kazoos; danced and listened to music by the Scottish rock groups Snow Patrol and Wet, Wet, Wet; drank cheap Scotch; mingled with loose women and even looser men; stared uninterruptedly at gigantic thermometers; welcomed residents from Brazil's rainforest and a bunch of occupants from frozen, treeless and rainless Tundra ecosystems which weather experts explain as "Holy cow, those are really freezing places especially atop bald mountains," held in Scotland earlier this week said today they were now in the

Ron Ruthfield

possession of a secret video taken during the main plenary session in which President Joe Biden was caught napping and almost falling on his COVID-masked nose smack on the table where he was sitting in a prone position with his arms symbolically crossed across his chest, his eyes automatically and effortlessly opening and closing like the electronic windows on the petrol-gulping 85-SUV parade taking him from the airport to his room at Motel 6 and perhaps dreaming about the melting glaciers in the Caribbean and Mediterranean Seas where he once frolicked with sharks, barracuda, Al Gore, and John Kerry, collectively, which revealed how swimmingly level-headed a president we actually have.

Via closed-circuit television broadcast in Nauru, The Isle of Wight (actual residents call it the Isle of White or Whyte), and Nepal, the speaker explained the reasons behind the leader of the free world intermittently snoozing and snoring his way to environmental victory with the emphasis on "mental."

"Hi, I'm Mike Lindell, your MyPillow guy," the video began. "I'm in Scotland right now and I'm so excited to tell you about two of my newest products that complement my pillows, Giza bed sheets made from Egyptian cotton by the very same workers who sculpted the Sphinx, towels, comforters, throw blankets, mattress toppers, men's and women's slippers, dog beds, adjustable beds, quilts, bathrobes, sleepwear, Bible story books, and fully adjustable lederhosen manufactured with materials directly from Tyrolean forests.

"While President Biden was in the Vatican meeting with the Pope, I was actually in Italy working on a new kind of pillow called the TushCush made from a brand-new discovery called Rome Foam. The prototype had just been completed when I caught a flight to Glasgow just in time for one of his

Ron Ruthfield

aides to place it on his chair as soon as the plenary session began.

"And an even bigger surprise for my customers is my announcement that MyPillow is enhancing all of our sleeping products by making MyPill, a new sleep aid and enhancer that has already been claimed an international success by testing it on the president at the Glasgow conference. Once his eyes started blinkin' – not to be confused with Secretary of State Antony Blinken – and yawning at least three times into his hand with his mouth covered, we knew we had another huge hit to add to our variety of products all produced in my home state of Minnesota.

"With these two new items, the one thing we can promise to consumers of MyPillow products is that we will never appeal to a Woke audience."

Ron Ruthfield

NAVY TAKES OVER ARMY, AIR FORCE, MARINES, COAST GUARD OPERATIONS

The Chairman of the United States military's Joint Chiefs of Staff, General Mark Milley, has announced he will be replaced by the youngest person – and the first female – to ever head America's armed forces. Milley is expected to retire next month unless he refuses to give up his post claiming that he fears leaving without his successor continuing his program of teaching Critical Race Theory, Drag Queen Philosophy, and Transgender Troop Systems to our military personnel throughout the world.

"This appointment is groundbreaking," Milley said, adding that the assignment is normally handled by the President "but in this case, there is a slight conflict of interest in that the appointee is related to Commander-In-Chief Joe Biden whose stunning military experience includes his heroic victory in

Ron Ruthfield

pulling U.S. troops out of Afghanistan one dead body at a time, and standing guard while roaming Rehoboth Beach, DE, at night looking for seashells and Nazi submarines.

"President Biden's 7th grandchild, Navy Roberts Biden, despite her being a mere four years old, has tremendous combat credentials, especially in the area of playing with floating plastic boats and beach landing craft while in the bathtub, and training to be America's first female Navy Seal while continuing on a diet of Ukrainian yogurt and Arkansas catfish." (This has actually been fact-checked by Snopes: the yogurt is a gift sent by Volodymyr Zelenskyy, President of Ukraine, and the seafood bill is being handled – without the slightest catch – by Hillary "Bottom Feeder" Clinton.)

In a bold effort to bring Navy, Hunter Biden's daughter into the family structure (some naysayers have floated the theory that the toddler was fathered by J. Edgar Hoover) President Biden is reported to have scribed a letter to his granddaughter while he was playing in the Oval Office with his 1979 Radio Shack computer and discovered by a White House staffer (the letter, not the president):

Ron Ruthfield

Dear Navy,

My, oh my, what a wonderful discovery to finally learn that you're my granddaughter. I've had a bunch of grandchildren, kiddo, because your daddy, my son Hunter, has played hanky-panky with more women than Wilt Chamberlain. Oh, that's right. You have no idea who Wilt Chamberlain was. In fact, I don't think you even know who your daddy is. Write me back and let me know because I'm interested in learning whether you'll carry the Biden name, thereby destroying the integrity of our entire family. And no, this isn't a joke. I'm not kidding! Hey, I'm pulling your leg, you little tyke. You know grandpa. Always proud of his kids and their offspring even if I've never known about you till today, or maybe it was four years ago. Who knows? It really doesn't matter unless you attempt to smear the family. Don't ever do that, Navy, or I swear I'll dump vanilla ice cream on your head. In public. Do you need more of a weekly allowance? Don't ask me for an increase. Ask your mom. Your father is in no position right now to give you an additional buck or two because of his financial, legal, and personal problems, although I will tell you he'd give you a 50% discount on one of his paintings. Be grateful, Navy. One day it'll be worth at least 3 shares of Burisma Oil. Now I'm not promising you anything, but if you ever get to visit me at the White House, I'll have Grandma Jill give you a full tour right after you grab an Uber from the Greyhound Bus Station. Just don't bring any baggies of cocaine with you even though your daddy does. Oh, never mind, you little squirt. Bring whatever the hell you want 'cause it'll be the one and only time you'll be here. Okay, I gotta go. And don't call me. I'm in no mood to create some bizarre relationship with you. Just remember, your grandma and grandpa love you just as much as we love your mom. By the way, did you know

Ron Ruthfield

she was arrested for prostitution but was back on the streets faster than your dad's last date?

We're sending you a lot of love. Don't use it up carelessly.

President Joe Biden (a/k/a Paw-Paw)

Navy will take on her top military assignment on January 1, 2024, or as soon as her mom dries her off after taking a bath.

NORTH KOREA ANNOUNCES SUICIDE BAN UNDER PENALTY OF DEATH

A spokesperson for the North Korean government has announced that the nation's military and policing authorities will shoot and kill any citizen who says he or she has the intent to commit suicide.

Oh Yoo-Suk, whose gender transition from a man to a woman was completed right after he ate his last plate of kimchi, said anyone caught thinking about purposely lowering North Korea's population growth, which last year was -9,105 citizens, will be hanged in public. According to sources who know Suk, North Koreans who have already committed suicide will be reawakened and poisoned to death with American-manufactured automobile additives so "… we can blame Uncle Sam on Auntie-Freeze."

Ron Ruthfield

At a formal press conference held near the demilitarized zone between Texas and Mexico, one Western reporter asked, "How will you know what citizens are thinking?"

"Ho Lee Kow," responded the spokesperson, "you stupid? Don't you know we invent Magic 8-ball?", adding that the hangings will be accompanied by exceptionally loud North Korean rap music, including "Killing Me Softly With Un's Song" which recently replaced "Live And Let Die" as the Hermit Kingdom's national anthem.

Kim Jong Un, Supreme Leader of North Korea and a man internationally known for his sparkling diplomacy, humor, superior intellect, hair style, golfing skills, and strict dietary discipline, told reporters that those "traitors who want commit suicide be dealt with no different many Bill and Hillary Clinton friends."

When asked to clarify that statement, Un asked, "You ever hear name Vince Foster, cousin of Stephen who thought Camptown Races run by here all da-do-da day? Both dead before 50 birthday!"

All 98 tourists who visited North Korea last year, according to official government statistics, threatened suicide after their first meal in the only 5-Star lodging facility, Motel 5 ½ in the nation's capital of Pyongyang, as rated by the People's Republic of Washington, D.C.

Although the actual number of annual suicides by North Koreans is a state secret, an informed government operative told me it was less than 25% of the murders on Chicago's south side during the past year, a tribute to all the hard work being done by North Korean authorities and former Chicago Mayor Lori Lightfoot.

Ron Ruthfield

Kim (no relation to Bassinger, Novak or Kardashian) is reported to have issued an emergency, secret directive that orders the beheading of local authorities who don't meet their quota of zero suicides per quarter for the next seven years, according to Radio Free Hollywood.

Taking your own life in North Korea is considered an act of treason against socialism, communism, statism, collectivism, Bolshevism, Globalism, Maoism, Taoism, Buddhism, Hinduism, Calvinism, Presbyterianism, Lutheranism, Atheism, Agnosticism, and Black Lives Matter.

Most of the suicides, according to unofficial statistics and analytics, are caused by severe poverty and starvation, and no one can come up with a countermeasure right now, according to the North Korean Department of Propaganda, a wholly owned division of the American Civil Liberties Union now operated and managed by Joy Reid of MSNBC fame.

In addition, those held accountable for skyrocketing suicides will be prevented forever from owning a Magic 8-ball.

Ron Ruthfield

NEW YORK POST ANNOUNCES WINNERS OF WHIMSICAL INTERNATIONAL COMPETITION

In an exciting and special print-run edition of the New York Post, the paper has declared three outstanding females as Global Jew-haters of the Year.

Editor's Note: At press time, personal pronoun choices by the trio were unknown but inside sources claimed they were Moe, Larry, and Curly.

"I'm thrilled to have been awarded this coveted title," said Dia Lupa, well-known British singing pop star whose memorable recordings of "I Left My Heart In Gaza" and the romantic ballad "I Love the Intifada, Too" earned her the honorary Yasser Arafat Trophy for Most Morally Corrupt Entertainer, which last year posthumously went to Richard Wagner, Hitler's favorite composer.

Ron Ruthfield

Our very own U.S. Congresswoman, Marjorie Taylor Greene (R-GA) picked up her Jew-hating award for the first time, although she has been entered in the festive occasion in past years. "I won, I won," she shouted to her adoring voter base as she broadly smiled while holding a huge black, red, and white flag adorned with bold lightning bolts that matched the armbands worn by most of the huge crowd of about 41 people in a field frequently used as a rallying point for the KKK, an organization mostly known for its charity work and placing a noose around the neck of Jussie Smollett, whose Jewish father has announced his progeny will fight the City of Chicago until he is vindicated or sent to prison, whichever comes first.

The Third Prize was not a surprise, especially among Israelis and your friendly correspondent who reported on this lady's activities a couple of months ago. Yes, it's one of the scoops of the year by the Post, naming Anuradha Mittal, Chairman of the Bored of Ben & Jerry's Ice Cream since 2008. Mittal, a recipient of the Official Pity Prize presented to her by the Zionist Organization of America in 2009 after one of its members spotted her handing out free pints of Hamas Hash and Monster Mash to Palestinian kids, has been accused of doling out tens of thousands in cash from the ice cream company's foundation to fund her own pro-Palestinian non-profit, namely the Jihadist-Peachy Peace Coalition.

The public might not know but there are 15 divisions in the global competition for Jew-hater of the Year Awards' program that began approximately 2,000 years ago:

Note the overlap in the six levels that includes Black Jewish Male and Female Politicians, which makes it enormously difficult for the judges to select the most outstanding among the various categories.

Ron Ruthfield

Also, the contestants will no longer compete in the swimsuit competition because, according to Rep. Ilhan Omar (D-MN), "Our bodies should only be seen by our husbands and brothers, especially by women if they are virgins above the age of 11."

Meanwhile, U.S. Vice-President Kamala Harris happily squeaked, "My husband is a Jew and we will not put up with the hatred unless former President Obama and ex-National Security Adviser Susan Rice say it's okay. Heh-heh-heh."

The tournament is fierce, and the international venues hosting the events spread from Florida to Tehran, and include the following categories:

1. Biggest Nose
2. Ugliest Kippah (skull cap)
3. Most Likely to Drink Christian Children's Blood
4. Alfred Dreyfus Look-Alike
5. Most Prolific Contributor to The Protocols of the Elders of Zion
6. Jews and Messianic Jews (Tied for 6th Place)
8. Those who appear to be Chosen
9. Notorious bankers
10. Hollywood propagandists
11. Females
12. Males
13. Blacks
14. Muslims
15. Politicians

Ron Ruthfield

Next year's contest, according to a Vatican spokesman, will be held in the Poodle Room of the Fontainebleau Hotel on Miami Beach. Tickets are on sale now and going fast. Get yours now at jewsarehorriblepeople.com.

Ron Ruthfield

U.S. CITIZENS GIVEN ONE WEEK BEFORE GOVERNMENT LOPS OFF GENITALIA

For the past month, while most of the nation was watching the Russians invade Ukraine leaving untold horrid carnage – which was almost as bad as Will Smith's whack across Chris Rock's kisser at the Academy Awards – the U.S. State Department has issued another policy that affects every man, woman, trans, gay, lesbian, binary, non-binary, cisgender, boy, girl, asexual, bisexual, gender fluid, gender expansive, gender queer, intersexual, pansexual, queer questioning, transitioning humans and pet goldfish.

As of this coming April, a spokesthing for the U.S. State Department has announced that from that date forward, the new policy – and I swear on everything that's holy and righteous, including the Boy Scout Oath (are the Boy Scouts still in business?) – that all citizens will have the ability to check and sign off the gender identification they would like printed

Ron Ruthfield

on their passports, passport cards, and emergency passports issued at embassies, consulates, and strip joints with pole dancers and massage parlors.

Assistant Deputy Director for Printing and Processing Official United States Identification, Dick Head, made the announcement from the department's field office in Moonbat, Alaska.

All one needs to do is mark a gender-neutral "X" on the form where it asks if the United States has lost its collective mind and – bingo! – you're in!

"Just know that your government is working hard on behalf of everyone who cares about justice and equity," Head said, adding that passports will no longer have to match the gender on your supporting documents such as a birth certificate, previous passport, state identification, medical documentation, elementary school library card, AARP membership card, or a wrist tattoo with your individual bar code in deep purple or navy blue, your choice.

Further, Head stated, the Transportation Security Administration (TSA) will no longer use magic wands to detect what your actual gender might be. "In other words," he added, "we are removing all lower-decker pecker-checkers from every airport in the nation and further asking all licensed pilots to remove them from their cockpits."

"No more pat downs," Head asserted. "They're too sensitive especially for those who might be wearing diaper bombs or a loaded Beretta Bobcat in their underwear."

Head made the announcement of the new policy on the eve of Transgender Day of Visibility, an annual event held on

Ron Ruthfield

March 31 that celebrates transgender persons, all while Americans were turning their attention to less important official agenda items, such as murder, rape, armed robbery, White House corruption, and the swarming of illegal immigrants at the Southern border of the U.S., including Canadians.

The U.S. special diplomatic envoy for LGBTQIA+ rights, a newly created position instituted by the Gay-Baptist-Muslim Alliance of America, will earn a commission on every new passport issued as of March 11 with an estimated personal income of $3.875 million the first operational year based on approximately 17.5 (not including children under six months old) million new immigrants who will swim or take a raft across the Rio Grande directly into Del Rio, Texas, unless they drown. No person, no commission.

"This marker," shouted the envoy into a megaphone blasting among a throng of 22 listeners in an Idaho potato field (and who does not want its name revealed; the envoy, not the megaphone) "is a huge and momentous step for everyone who actually cares about administrative systems and policies that account for the diversity of gender identity, gender expression, and sexual characteristics among U.S. citizens and Californians.

But the reason few Americans know about the new Gender X policy, according to Head, is that the megaphone's button was in the off position, no different than the common malady among bureaucrats of paying no attention to the dangers of screwing with someone's sex.

Ron Ruthfield

PRESIDENT BIDEN SECRETLY CALLS PRIME MINISTER NETANYAHU ON BURNER PHONE

In what can only be described as a high-level intercept operation, an intelligence officer and spokesman for the Mossad, Israel's crack spy agency, announced late today it had intercepted and recorded a phone call from U.S. President Joe Biden to Prime Minister Benjamin Netanyahu.

"Actually, the Prime Minister has been waiting for a call since President Biden was sworn in on January 20, but the way this call was initiated was highly unusual," the officer said. "The frequency of the communications line showed evidence that someone – we had no idea who it was – was attempting an unconventional way to reach Prime Minister Netanyahu, and we had just enough time to hook up an electronic device to record the conversation.

Ron Ruthfield

"Hello, Bibi, baby? This is Joe."

"Joe? Joe who? You mean Yossi?"

"Come on, man. It's Joe. Joe Biden. Listen, pal, I didn't mean to have you wait so long for a call. We had you listed at 104th to give you a ring but you know how things can get bogged down. I had to call Abbas to tell him I sent him a few hundred million shekels so they could pay their guys in Israeli prisons. I was told he was actually at his bank in Switzerland and so darn tough to get a hold of. I'm prioritizing as best I can. Anyway, I'm on one of those throw-up phones so no one really knows I'm touching base with you."

"Throw-up phones? You mean throw-away phones?"

"Come on, Bibi. You know what I'm talkin' about, you little grammarian Hebe. Hey, I need a favor. Can you get your folks out of the Golan Heights for a short period of time, like a decade?"

"For what purpose, Joe?"

"Well, I need some leverage with the Iranians. Malley and Sherman and Haines and Blinken and the rest of my Jew-crew need to give the mullahs something – anything in return for our dealing with them and returning to the agreement we had with them."

"I'm afraid I can't do that, you dog-faced pony soldier."

"Well, then, maybe you can pull out of Gaza."

"Actually, we left Gaza 16 years ago but in the event you didn't know, we're now at war with Hamas in the Gaza Strip."

Ron Ruthfield

"What?? Nobody told me! Come on, man. Hey, when I was in Gaza City, I couldn't even go to a 7-Eleven or a Dunkin' Donuts unless I had a slight Arabic accent. And I'm not joking. Listen, Bibi. Think it over and let me know. Meantime, say hello to Sadie for me."

"My wife's name is Sara, Joe. And by the way, give my best wishes to Jill."

"That would be DOCTOR Jill, Bibi."

"Come for a visit, Joe. I'd like to personally thank you for taking the helm of President Obama's third term."

Ron Ruthfield

PUTIN: THE MUSICAL

While the Russian military machine continues to pound Ukraine and kill innocent civilians, including children, President Vladimir Putin's press secretary in a strange move has announced the creation of what has the makings of a Broadway blockbuster.

"We hope to have 'Putin: The Musical', finished by May 1, International Workers Day. With the generous help of American Democratic Socialists, Cuban and Venezuelan musicians and others in the worldwide Communist Creative Community, the Stolichnaya Utopian Theater in Moscow will present, in Broadway terms, "another opening, another show" as a musical tribute and friendly gesture to Volodymyr Zelenskyy, president of Ukraine.

Now that certainly struck the right note among the press with the New York Times running a front-page headline: SEE, WE TOLD YOU THE ROOSKIES ARE IN TUNE WITH AMERICA.

Ron Ruthfield

"President Putin wants to edify the world that Russians across 11 time zones are peaceful and only want tranquility and harmony for all people, except for the rest of Europe, the United States, and a number of archipelagos in the Caribbean, including Jeffrey Epstein's Pedophile Island," the Kremlin statement said.

Prior to Zelenskyy's political career, he was a well-known television comedy star and won the Ukrainian version of Dancing With The Tsars. Kremlin press personnel commented that in Putin: The Musical, Zelenskyy will be reviving the famous George Gershwin tune, "They Can't Take That Away from Me, Especially Kiev."

Should Zelenskyy's military troops begin to cave under the heavy-handed and brutal Russian invasion of his nation of more than 40 million, he will add a second number, "Let's Call the Whole Thing Off" from Gershwin's Broadway show, "Shall We Dance" which was the #1 best-selling recording in the Soviet Union in June 1941 when what the Nazis called Operation Barbarossa invaded St. Petersburg.

It proved to be a massive defeat for Germany not realizing the city was in Russia, not the west coast of Florida where the elderly go to die. Too bad their troops struck a bad chord when they dressed in polyester leisure suits and golf hats and arrived in Volga convertibles instead of putting on camouflage uniforms, steel helmets, and jumping into their Panzers.

According to White House sources, U.S. President Joe Biden was thrilled to hear about the Russian gesture with American overtones and has agreed to perform in the opening night of the musical by singing Bob Hope's "Tanks for the Memories" if the Commander-in-Chief can remember the

Ron Ruthfield

words. Otherwise, he will simply be placed at stage left – far left – while he sits on President Putin's lap as the Russian leader pulls the strings while Biden remains in puppet mode.

The show, said the press release, is scheduled to run for 90 nights or until the theater is burned down or bombed by Russian militants, whichever comes first.

Tickets, which start at 1 ruble, can be purchased by calling toll-free 800-COS-SACK. Theatergoers are being told to wait until the inflation continues to spiral out of control in Russia so that the theater will actually pay patrons to attend the show.

Sounds like music to my ears.

TOP 5 REASONS WHY QUEEN ELIZABETH PASSED AWAY SO YOUNG

As much as she struggled to reach the century mark, Queen Elizabeth II, Ruler of the United Kingdom, except for San Francisco and Wyoming, simply couldn't accelerate the horse-drawn royal carriage to meet her goal of living 100 years.

Upon her passing, former U.S. President William Jefferson Clinton remarked about the Queen missing her 100th birthday, "Close, but no cigar."

According to a panel of regal authorities in the fields of aristocracy, nobility, and bangers and who kept in close contact with the queen's 232 Doctors of the Realm, they have put forth the 5 Top Reasons why her highness met her ultimate demise four years too early.

1. "First and foremost," suggested Sir Stetson Headley, "her tiaras weighed an average of 52 pounds and 12 shillings. She wore one virtually every time she left one of her 190

Ron Ruthfield

palaces, castles, mansions, fortresses, chateaus, homes, Jeffrey Epstein's Caribbean island, and her 3-bedroom, 2 1/2-bath residence in Boca Raton, Florida." The headpieces caused her a lifetime of neck pain and curvature of the spine resulting in severe stenosis. He added, "Yes, you might have thought she was smiling all of the bloody time but if you look closely at old photos, it was actually a facial grimace, although she did brush her teeth regularly using Crest with a fluoride additive."

2. She wore too many hats with feathers, noted her allergist, Dr. Ima Sneezy. "I told her on many occasions that she's allergic to quills and to be extra careful with the pleasant pheasants, but like all royals, she did not take me seriously. After careful analysis, wearing the feathers took approximately 37 hours off her life as a direct result of her wheezing from the pollen attracted to the plumes."

3. The Queen's staff of more than 12-dozen personal chefs, which equals the number of employees at a 3-story McDonald's, mentioned she ate too many crumpets, scones, and haggis the last two months of her life. I mean eating the heart, liver, and lungs of a sheep with minced onion, oatmeal, suet, mixed with spices and salt and cooked while encased in the animal's stomach could kill a human faster than a rocket lobbed by Hamas at an Israeli kibbutz.

4. Lizzie, as she liked to be called by close friends, knew if she passed on to the great citadel in the sky before President Biden, she would force him to attend her funeral and thereby cause a diplomatic coup. And she was correct. Biden, barring any claims he might make about oversleeping and not having enough time to make it aboard

Ron Ruthfield

Air Farce One to attend the service and interment, balked at showing up saying to one reporter that if he goes to London, he might wind up on top of a statue column in Trafalgar Square or headless if he unknowingly wandered into a no-go zone. After having his daily tantrum, he agreed to attend the funeral as long as there wasn't enough space for two at the gravesite hole.

5. The queen's brain cells had been swirling for many years because try as she would, she simply couldn't recall all the nations of which she ruled over. In fact, she had more titles than the Library of Congress. The brain strain finally took its toll. Hey, if you were a King, Queen, Prince, Princess, Duke, Duchess, Lord, Lordette, a Royal Highness, Defender of the Faith, Queen of Scots and Scotch, or Meghan Markle's grandmother-in-law you'd have a tough time, too.

Beginning Sunday, September 11 (don't remind me of you-know-what), the Queen's body will be schlepped from Balmoral Castle in Edinburgh, Scotland, to at least 40 more of her residences, 30 churches, and of course the Bevis Marks Synagogue in London where the temperatures have plunged to record lows. So, there's a good chance we will have to watch them sit 'n shiver.

But the 70-year record-run Queen Elizabeth had made her eminently qualified to share some outstanding memories in the company of Winston Churchill and Margaret Thatcher.

Jack the Ripper? Not so much.

Ron Ruthfield

OFFICIAL LIST OF ITEMS FOUND IN "CONFIDENTIAL" BOXES AT MAR-A-LAGO, A/K/A UNCLE DON'S VILLAGE

Possessing the vast amount of important and highly placed government contacts (the number varies between one and two, including a post office letter carrier), your friendly reporter has seized an official list of items poached by the FBI at the Palm Beach bungalow colony of former President Donald Trump.

All of the materials absconded with by the Biden Administration's operatives are part of the newly revised security classifications of top-secret, middle-secret, bottom-secret, furtively secret, not-so-secret, and "Hey, you, don't open this box"-secret classifications, all with the approbation and canonization of Attorney General Merrick Garland. The new lexicon of levels has been revised for the first time since Benedict Arnold was a pharmacist.

Ron Ruthfield

One box stuffed with the same message on each of the 1,000 sheets of paper was imprinted with "ORANGE MAN DID NOT PACK THE BOXES" in all capital letters and printed in Republican Red in Brandon Grotesque 72-point typeface.

Also included was a complete list of 87,000 new IRS agents typed in alphabetical order, including requests to the government by every agent to provide them with their weapon of choice, including a wide selection of 9MM Glocks; Smith & Wesson Model 60; .357 Magnums; Beretta 21A Bobcats, 418s and 950s; Makarov semi-automatics made in the Soviet Union; Daniel Boone-era muskets; and daggers hand-crafted by Islamic radicals.

Three additional laptop computers once owned by Hunter Biden with all pornography and hard drives, in fact, intact, were also retrieved and cushion-packed with jumbo-sized, zip-tied baggies of cocaine. Additionally, one of the agents hand-counted 47 expired, round-trip tickets to Kiev valid for Hunter Biden which were purchased by Burisma, an obscure Ukrainian oil company that no one in the current federal government ever heard of.

One of the major discoveries in two of the boxes included an assortment of U.S. Representative (D-NY) Gerald Nadler's girdles and lap bands with original sales tags indicating that the congressman from New York bought the items in the same store where Monica Lewinsky purchased a blue dress some years ago.

Another box contained a horse's head with a note between its teeth saying, "Insert under bed blanket of my look-alike lawmaker Marxist Alexandra Ocasio-Cortez, the former

Ron Ruthfield

mixologist of Harvey Wallbangers and Comfortable Screws (a mixture of Southern Comfort and orange juice)." **Editor's Note:** At press time, AOC had not been informed about the head-in-the-bed.

One of the agents took issue with the descriptions comparing the equine's head and teeth with the same physical traits of the New York member of the House Select Committee on Barkeeping even though he was informed that the horse and the horse's ass had been on the same diet of oats and hay for years.

Another cardboard container held hundreds of photocopies of the Steele Dossier, the highly credible and fully responsible, not to mention patriotic, report that linked President Trump with Russian operatives and the Duma to help the commissars in Moscow gain leverage in the White House. The dossier was funded by the Hillary Clinton presidential campaign, and the moment it was published was considered as sacred to the Democratic Party as the Bible (Old and New Testaments plus the Miscellaneous Garments for Sale in the classified ad section), Das Kapital, and the Communist Manifesto.

One of the major surprises, my contact said, was the extra-short incarceration diary of Jeffrey Epstein, plus his last will and testament showing he left his entire estate to the Girl Scouts of America. (You're probably aware that Girl Scout cookies by the container load are now being sold exclusively by the Transgender Coalition of Non-binary Athletes which recently merged with the Girl Scouts and Brownies). An undercover operative let it slip that in the very same box were thousands of wallet-size photos of Bill Cosby.

Ron Ruthfield

In another well-secured and padded carton, agents found 14 designer crack pipes from the colorful collections of Hunter Biden and the 13 hookers he slept with on January 6, 2021, inside the U.S. Capitol right behind the still-standing statue of Robert E. Lee. Apparently, the Capitol Police were too busy fighting off insurrectionists to notice the president's son in his natural habitat.

Surprisingly, two C-17 Globemaster troop transport aircraft used to move U.S. military personnel in and out of Afghanistan, each folded perfectly (the planes, not the troops) so that they all fit into one banker's box. Also included were the dusty remains of five Afghans who were found frozen hanging onto the wings of both planes. According to an inside source, the FBI found 50 fingernails still attached to one of the folded wings and didn't really take up much room in the treasure trove of discoveries. The box also included an invoice from the Department of Justice for the cost of the planes and addressed to the Mar-A-Logo Activities Director, Oprah Winfrey.

Also found were thousands of 5"x 7" glossy color photos of former President Trump and erstwhile Prime Minister of Israel, Benjamin Netanyahu, all personally signed by both men to hand out at the next Democrat Socialist Party convention, as well as to officials of the Jewish Republican Coalition.

Detailed architectural plans and renderings were found for the President Joseph Biden LieBerry, which is scheduled to be built at Guantanamo Bay within three months from the date the president can no longer open his eyes, which actually is tomorrow. The time frame has been set by professional medical personnel who have projected that the president's drooling will become dramatically noticeable by that time, and that he will

Ron Ruthfield

have to have his shoelaces tied by a U.S. Coast Guardsman well trained in fastening knots.

Lastly, three boxes of overripe plantains were located, indicating that the United States of America is now being considered for immediate membership on the United Nations' official list of banana republics.

Olé, Jose.

Ron Ruthfield

RITTENHOUSE NOMINATED FOR PRESIDENCY OF BLACK LIVES MATTER

The international organization of Black Lives Matter (And White Lives Don't) has unanimously selected Kyle Rittenhouse who only last week was acquitted of the killing of two men and wounding a third during the peaceful torching, sabotaging, and looting of Kenosha, WI, in August 2020 by church-going youth, as head of its global empire.

In addition, George Zimmerman has been named Director of Cracka' Outreach by the pacifist organization, according to sources who also asserted that Zimmerman's office will be outfitted with life-size statues of Trayvon Martin and OJ Simpson, both of which are currently being sculpted by the same artist who designed and created the Titanic and likenesses of George Floyd who, as you know unless you were hiding in a cave in Vietnam's Ha Long Bay, died by a knee-to-the-neck by

Ron Ruthfield

a Minneapolis police officer in May 2020 and whose number of icons has now surpassed 5,800 bronze, marble, clay, and reclaimed plywood now scattered across the United States – excluding the city of Floyd, VA – and parts of Antarctica where Emperor penguins have been discovered creating likenesses of Floyd from ice, snow, and plastic from assorted six-pack rings of Samuel Adams Winter Lager, Coors Light, and Bud Ice.

"Kyle is the kind of young man who we hold in high esteem," said Patrice Khan-Cullors, the ex-executive director of the Black Lives Matter Global Network Foundation who issued a statement from one of her four, multi-million dollar Red Army estates which according to Zillow real estate estimates are now collectively worth more than the entire GDP of Tonga and Vermont.

"Being a communist, anti-Semite, anti-white, anti-Zionist, and anti-American doesn't mean I can't enjoy the fruits of others' labors while I take care of the roses in my gardens," she commented liltingly and rhapsodically while at the same time voicing her approval of Rittenhouse's actions by declaring, "What a great shot Kyle is! Too bad he wasn't with us in Ferguson."

Khan-Cullors stepped down from her position as head of the organization, a controversial move some say, to devote much of her time, she claimed, to build a worldwide network BLM /Marxist /Islamist Homes for Israeli and Jewish Orphans (BLMIHIJO). Colleagues suspect she grabbed some cash from the BLM till to begin to build its first orphanage on the South Side of Chicago where she announced, "The kids will be safe in that neighborhood." Other homes, she said, are being planned for Khartoum, Tehran, and Havana.

Ron Ruthfield

After accepting the top-dog position, Rittenhouse exclaimed, "Wow! Anyone in the club named Silverman?"

Ron Ruthfield

PRESIDENT ISSUES EXECUTIVE ORDERS WHILE EATING CRANBERRY SAUCE

In the middle of Thanksgiving dinner (actually it was during the 9th course and immediately prior to a choice of 50 desserts, one for each state including Beverly Hills) at the home of President Biden's longtime friend and mega-donor, David Rubenstein whose multi-jillion-dollar (in today's currency roughly six trillion Chinese Yuan) compound in Nantucket, MA, is five acres larger than Florida's Lake Okeechobee and has more square footage than the Pentagon which next year is being converted into a warehouse for weapons returned to the U.S. military by Afghanistan's Taliban except for the 174 aircraft, 64,343 machine guns, 126,295 hand guns, and 169 tanks left behind which will be used, according to official sources in the Defense Department, as a gift to Haibatullah Askhunzada, Supreme Leader of the Taliban People's Peace

Ron Ruthfield

Movement and Shooting Gallery, announced he had signed a number of Executive Orders.

Rubenstein, whose now-deceased cousin Helena simply made it up as she went along in the lipstick business and whose beauty rivaled that of a horseshoe bat, declared that his property – note the quote marks which means he actually said this! – "…approximates the land mass that the State of Delaware occupies not including the guest house…" in which the president drafted the EOs that he wrote with the help of his son, Hunter who had just finished another painting commissioned by the President's official sign-language interpreter who held up the middle finger on his right hand to indicate he only wanted one.

President Biden noted that because he personally had to spell out the exact language in the various EOs, he brushed up on his spelling by taking the course, Hooked on Phonics, prior to his trip to Nantucket.

The Commander-in-Chief additionally announced that he had signed another EO that had approval from the Democratic Party, including Sen. Ted Kennedy (D-MA), and the Federal Reserve which is mandating a currency switch whereby the U.S. dollar will officially become the U.S. Kopek – named after Kennedy's one-night girlfriend, Mary Joe Kopechne whose unsuccessful attempt to swim in Chappaquiddick's Poucha Pond below the Dike Bridge (which had nothing to do with Kennedy's sex life) on the eastern end of Martha's Vineyard ended in her demise after the senator's automobile, all by itself, decided to swerve off the span because, based on reports by Kennedy himself, "It needed water for its radiator."

Ron Ruthfield

Another Executive Order issued by President Biden states that every U.S. embassy and consulate in the entire world will not only fly the American flag but the Rainbow flag as well. In addition, the president has changed the national anthem from The Star-Spangled Banner to Somewhere Over the Rainbow with lyrics other than those sung by Judy Garland but which have been rewritten and updated by her great nephew, Merrick Garland. "Flying just below the Rainbow flag will be a black one with hu-u-u-ge white letters representing BLM" which, according to Biden, represents the Bureau of Land Management.

"Additional Executive Orders numbering in the thousands are forthcoming," said Chief of Staff Ron Klain. "The president believes that the nation hasn't experienced enough hope and change because of the previous administration's arrogance and malfeasance."

An unidentified staffer remarked, "That comment is a distinct voice from a cranberry bog."

Ron Ruthfield

SEATTLE HERE WE COME

So, the wife and I were talking a couple of days ago, which is itself a minor miracle after three months in quarantine.

"Geez, after such a long time being stuck in the house, I think we need to get away for a long weekend somewhere," she admonished, although some might call it nagging.

"Sure, sweetheart," a reference normally saved for when I've done something wrong which is why I call her "sweetheart" on an hourly or even more-often basis. "Where would you like to go, sweetheart?"

"Well, I was thinking since we've recently been in Costa Rica and Florida, I'd like to go somewhere different. Like Seattle."

"SEATTLE, sweetheart??? Have you lost your mind, SWEETHEART? Don't you know what's going on in Seattle, SWEETTHEARTTTT?" as I calmly tried to explain the carved out enemy territory in a six-square-block area of the Emerald

Ron Ruthfield

City's downtown. "Are you aware, sweetheart, that the Huns have set up shop in CHAZ, now called CHOP?"

Whaddaya mean CHOP? You mean like a CHOP shop?"

"Not exactly, SWEETHEART. It's more like if you look at them the wrong way, they'll chop off your head. I mean we're talking HUNS!"

I decided to make a call to the CHOP Tourism Department to get the facts.

"Hi, my wife and I are confirmed atheists without an agenda – and by the way, we detest capitalism, love to read poetry by Karl Marx, Vlad Lenin, and Jane Fonda and we'd like to visit your new town." I was hoping that whichever young lady I was talking to would provide me with critical information. And Olga, who sounded as though a previous job she held must have been that of a whip-equipped prison guard at the luxurious, 5-Star Stasi Prison in East Berlin, certainly did.

"You'll need a visa. $100 each. We take MasterRaceCard and Antifa Express. I can take down the information now and email valid documents. You'll have exactly 24 hours to stay in CHOP, then go back across the border making sure you have your papers stamped at our Visa Tent. If you're late leaving, it will cost another minimum fee of $100 per person plus a modest donation for our free-range chicken farm and sprout garden. The tent is yellow and blue and just to the far, far left (where else would it be?) of the Official Proletariat Entrance. The one with the urine stains on all four sides. Just walk around the feces fences."

"Any restaurants in CHOP?"

Ron Ruthfield

"Yeah, a Soviet-style cafeteria specializing in borscht and mutton, and a Chinese haunt that serves CHOP SUEY and Mongolian beef cooked by Chef Attila." There it was. The clue that the HUNS were actually going to cook our food! Or us.

"What sleeping accommodations do you have for one elderly couple? We'll need a handicapped room, of course."

"How old are you," she inquired, hinting that a two-person pup tent was available for $195 a night plus tax and resort service fee.

"You'll see it on my visa and passport," I said quite firmly, knowing that I might never be allowed to step foot in the capitalist-free zone. I was a bit dejected knowing that my wife and I would probably be issued a "No Entry" stamp and by default could never be official CHOPPERS. That appellation would only be applicable as a result of having false teeth.

"If you're old and white, don't bother to come," she ordered. "Our friendly staff is in no mood to be bothered by racists."

I hung up the phone, turned to my wife, and said, "Let's pass on Seattle, sweetheart. We'll go to temple this Shabbat and pray about Jacob and his beautiful tents, a much more bountiful respite that keeps us at a distance from acne-faced, black-masked, inhuman rubbish."

Ron Ruthfield

DON'T JUDGE ME BY MY SKIN COLOR BUT BY THE COLOR OF MY TEETH

Why would any person born with light skin, also described as light white, medium white, and heavily white people with origins in the Caucuses, feel guilty about not having enough melanin pigment embedded in their epidermis to appear darker without having to use Coppertone with an SPF of less than 10, a query which can be forwarded to Rachel Dolezal, America's Black-and-White Princess?

Why would "white" be considered an insult to people of color and an abundance of whites when George Floyd's funeral cortege was led by three white caissons, adorned by all-white flowers rolling along on white wheels and being pulled by six white horses?

Why would any sane businessperson – small, medium, or large – no matter what his or her skin color might be open or reopen a retail, commercial, or office building enterprise in a

Ron Ruthfield

city where rampaging animals duplicate the running of the bulls in Pamplona and replicated Cossacks sacking Ukrainian villages?

Why would anyone agree with the disgraceful acts of moral cowardice and bankruptcy by the collaborating Democrat Marxists, who are now in feckless obeisance to their most odious, radical, and bigoted members driven by some totalitarian and anti-Semitic ideology?

Why would any sanctimonious circus clown permit a societal wretch named Alfred Charles Sharpton, Jr., who was likely ordained in a rat-infested toilet in a Harlem crack house, preside over Mr. Floyd's funeral, thereby exacerbating the race-baiting and Jew-hating calumnies embedded within the African American community and especially in the ideological portfolio of Black Lives Matter?

Why would any American forget about the total lack of moral probity and clarity, irrespective of religious faith or political allegiance, especially when they vote in November?

And why would I – an absolutely wonderful person who has nothing but goodwill toward anyone who does not agitate me – apologize for anything I have not done? Indeed, I am declaring right here and right now that when you look at my receding hairline toward the front of my head, you might see not a symbol of atonement for some racial sin, but a great, big imaginary billboard telling Antifa, Black Lives Matter, Nancy Pelosi, Chuck Schumer, AOC, Jamaal Bowman, Rashida Tlaib, and the Congressional chick from Somalia, and the rest of the kneeling, toxic, querulous windbags they can all take long walks on short piers.

Ron Ruthfield

If I sound somewhat obstreperous, I am. Most especially toward an ample number of people in the greater sclerotic Jewish American community whose ubiquitous and masochistic calls for Social Justice and Repairing the World continue to resonate with fewer and fewer of their brothers and sisters.

We'd like some justice, too!

Ron Ruthfield

SO NICE TO MEAT YOU

Yes, another major miracle has occurred in the Middle East; one which equals the first successful baptism of a feral cat. Finally, the Palestinians and their avid supporters in Europe, the United States, Canada, Venezuela, and the United Nations have now discovered that the evil Jews in Israel have been training cattle to spy on their activities. Especially the bovines who graduated cum laude from the Massachusetts Institute of Technology with advanced degrees in Surveillance, Algorithms and Little Dogie Physics.

Some of them also earned advanced degrees from Israel's Technion University, matriculating the likes of Elsie the Borden Cow, and Minnie Moo, a famous Holstein cow at Disney World whose claim to fame was having spots shaped like Mickey Mouse on her side but in reality, was an operative in Israel's finest commando unit, Sayeret Matkal. Minnie Moo's bravery in gathering sensitive intelligence has enabled the Israeli Defense Force, with pinpoint accuracy, to identify

Ron Ruthfield

Palestinian terrorists attempting to spread the new strain of COVID named COWVID within heavily populated areas. "We made sure to educate our cows and bulls when they were young, and even threw in some high-IQ bison" said the co-directors of the Israeli Ministry of Heifers, Oprah Winfrey and Stacy Abrams whose birth name is Abramowitz. Both are two of the world's leading experts on Cattle Sexuality, Weight Loss, Animal Porn, and Bovine Depression.

"From our decades of work in Animal Husbandry, we knew we could educate Minnie Moo. Besides, we were 99% certain we could train cattle (with three or four hoofs) with or without horns and turn them into a special investigative black-and-white unit of Holstein Mossad agents."

Spokesmen for the Palestinian Authority in Ramallah and Hamas in Gaza have finally located the major source of information leaks from a Jewish Guernsey and they're milking it for all their worth. However, according to the source, they're cows and bulls giving us the information. But not just any regular type.

"These particular brands of bovines are highly trained even to the point where they not only use binoculars but also are nimble enough to wear night-vision goggles for scrutinizing Palestinian villages and individual Bedouin tents," commented Ibn Bam-Boozled who was recently released from a Jerusalem mental hospital for running around a cattle corral in an attempt to mount a gay bull. From the front. "Those demented Zionist butchers are even permitting government-owned herds to go to the Temple Mount in an effort to destroy Al Aqsa Mosque!" exclaimed Moomoo bin Dairi, an Arab grifter and ex-communicated imam who was recently accused of attempting to milk 72 cows without a halal pail. His defense team told the

Ron Ruthfield

court he confused the 72 pails with which they caught him with 72 virgins and only meant to squeeze milk from a maximum of 10 bulls.

"Just like the Jews," bin Dairi said, "they all had horns." A Sharia Court in Jericho heard the case and gave him a harsh but appropriate sentence: No more cookies with his goat milk for the next five years, including the breaking of the fast after Ramadan.

When asked what Palestinians would do if they wrangled some of the cattle and actually fed some poor Palestinian families whose sons, brothers, fathers, uncles, and cousins were in Israeli prisons, bin Dairi uttered, "I don't really know. I'm a vegetarian myself."

Ron Ruthfield

SOCIAL MEDIA EXECS ANNOUNCE DRAMATIC SHIFT TO ANTI-SOCIAL MEDIA

The heads of the biggest three social media platforms in the world (excluding the Pitcairn Islands and Moscow, Idaho) appeared today before the U.S. Senate Commerce Committee.

Speaking from various locations via remote connections such as individual senator's playrooms, bathrooms, and tree houses, it had been rumored that one of them would not be able to appear to question the trio of techies. Later, reliable sources said the missing senator was found with Hunter Biden's laptop attempting to erase several pornography sites. Although he went unnamed, the senator is believed to be married to a certain "Mrs. Blumenthal."

Citing Section 230 of the Communications Decency Act of 1996, considered a legal shield enacted to protect start-up

Internet companies from liability, a senator asked the head of Google, Sundar Pichai, why the legislation should not be changed and if he can change his name to a more pronounceable moniker to the average American parrot.

"Changing it now would violate my rights. I've always had season tickets in Section 230, Row A, Seats 1, 2, 3 and 4. Why would I want to change them? Seating rights come under the Civil Rights Act of 1964! Why would a U.S. senator deny me and my family the ability to keep those tickets in perpetuity at Levi's Stadium even though I only have 138 pairs of jeans in every color?"

Another senator asked Twitter's former CEO, Jack Dorsey (no relation to Tommy or Jimmy) why his firm continually allowed Holocaust denial to be posted. "Wouldn't that fall into the category of Fake News?" queried the lawmaker.

"Actually, that more likely falls into the category of Fake Jews," answered Herr Dorsey whose family changed its last name from Goebbels when they immigrated to the United States from Germany in 1946.

"Can you tell this committee why Twitter refused to allow users to post the post by the New York Post posting the already posted news that presidential candidate Joe Biden's son, Hunter, had left his computer at a repair shop and never picked it up? And that the hard drive contained information that linked Joe to shady foreign business deals in Ukraine and China while he was Vice-President of the United States? And that the hard drive is now in the hands of the FBI? And that the entire world is waiting for your answer?"

"I'll get back to you on that," Dorsey answered as spittle dripped on his beard. "Wanna do lunch on Election Day?"

Ron Ruthfield

Mark Zuckerberg, the co-founder and chief titan of Facebook, was asked about his company's role in stifling free speech.

"It is a particularly tricky problem to find the specific calibration in proportional timing that would be appropriate to stem the acceleration of speech created by those whose political failings might prematurely abort the decline in the ratios of the Al Gore rhythms we use to allow people to express their opinions no matter what the subject might be," Zuckerberg said.

"Finally," replied the senator from Guam, "we have some clarity."

Ron Ruthfield

STOP MAKING FUN OF PRESIDENT GUMP

My Mama always told me life is like a box of secret documents because you never know what you're gonna get. And Mama always had a way of explaining to me so I could understand everything.

She always told me that if you possess those secrets on paper, you should make something creative out of them. So, I did. In fact, Mama told me to do the best with what God gave me. So, I took up Japanese Origami and made lots of birds out of them and sent them flying into the air all over the place and where everybody got one, including the President of the United States who I was named after, Forrest Gump Biden.

Funny thing, my best good friend Bubba told me he saw some of the paper birds land in a garage right behind a 1967 Corvette somewhere in Delaware. Bubba also told me some of 'em wound up in a Delaware beach house. Mama told me to

Ron Ruthfield

stay away from Delaware because she never much liked the politicians who live in that state. Mama was right. Mama was always right.

I don't know if we each have a destiny or if we're all just floating around accidental, like on a breeze. But I think maybe it's both. Maybe both are happening at the same time. I mean my Origami birds flew all over the place and lots of people won't keep it a secret if they unfold my Japanese handiwork and read what's on 'em. Like my girlfriend Jenny Curran used to say. "Dear God, make me a bird. So, I could fly far. Far, far away from here."

I suppose Mama and Jenny knew a lot of things. "Stupid is as stupid does," Mama always used to tell me. Especially when crackheads are living in big mansions with their mommas and poppas.

But I did like visiting the White House and meeting Presidents JFK, LBJ, and Richard Nixon. The best thing about visiting a President is the food! Now, since it was all free, and I wasn't hungry but thirsty, I must've drunk me 15 Dr. Peppers. After my last visit, Bubba – and Bubba was never wrong – told me that many classified documents were kept at the University of Pennsylvania Center for Diplomacy and Global Engagement. Now why anybody would leave those kinds of papers at a university is a question that only Mama could probably answer. But Mama passed a long time ago and I can't ask her. Mama always said dying was a part of life. I sure wish it wasn't. Mama also said you've got to put the past behind you before you can move on.

Ron Ruthfield

I guess I'll have to wait until Forrest Gump Biden answers so many questions. He might even invite me to pay him a visit. In prison.

Ron Ruthfield

STUDENT CHICKENS CRY FOWL

As of this writing, the entire nation except for the last Top 10 winners of Jeopardy! (who are trying to discern why guest host Mayim Bialik wears authentic thrift shop outfits left over from Eleanor Roosevelt's wardrobe), have figured out that the Supreme Court has saved the nation's taxpayers at least $108.00 for the next fiscal year.

In a 6-3 opinion this past week, the highest court in the land who regularly smoke pot which is why – I swear I'm not making this up – it's called the highest court, announced that college and university students are going to have to pay up on their student loans or surrender their graduation certificates to illegal immigrants and forfeit their Volvos to the U.S. Government Motor Pools which have nothing to do with swimming or large bodies of water.

Mega-qualified, certified financial analysts who sometimes speak English and understand how to add and subtract, although some failed on their multiplication tables and division

Ron Ruthfield

scores in graduate school, have posited that the savings to taxpayers are what one called "Bunyanesque" which immediately sent the White House Communications Chief scurrying to upload his computer's thesaurus.

"The budget will reflect a savings of approximately $108, which in 1953 terms means at least $812," said Earnest Money, an Assistant's Assistant to the Assistant Secretary of Student Loans for the University of Truth or Consequences, New Mexico.

Offsetting the savings will be a fiscal budget for next year of $468.97 trillion, some earmarked for Congressional and Executive Branch junkets to investigate what President Biden has called "Russia's war with Iraq."

In this correspondent's effort to get a reading from student-loan borrowers, he got in his Volvo and traveled to Boston, Massachusetts, to interview some of the brightest and best scholars in the nation, many of whom attend outstanding educational institutions such as MIT, Boston University, Boston College, Harvard, and Pilgrim Preparatory School whose mascot is a turkey but looks and squawks like a chicken.

"I cry fowl," said Bessie Mae Mucho, a native of Toad Suck, Arkansas, who majors in Gay Duck Grooming at Harvard. "I'm back in the debt coop for $390,000, a mere portion of what I owe in student loans. There's no way I can pay that money back until I get my Ph.D. in Advanced Pheasantry and Peacock Preening. The six justices of the Supreme Court who took away our money," she added, while tears fell from her cheeks and were immediately licked and swallowed by a home of nearby pigeons, "should be tarred and feathered and run out of the nation's capital."

Ron Ruthfield

With equal anger and frustration, your always-friendly-unless-I-don't-like-you correspondent interviewed a student from Middlesex County Community College in nearby Bedford. A school official who asked for Ann O'nymity (Ann was on vacation at the time) shall remain nameless for what he called an "intrusive assault on the integrity of our 134 students' bank accounts and wallets. Their average $197.00 loans aren't exactly chicken feed."

Unfortunately, no one else from Harvard, MIT, or any other institution of higher learning in the Boston area would even comment on the Supreme Court decision.

They were too busy standing in line for their lunch at the closest Chick-Fil-A and Buffalo Wild Wings franchises.

Ron Ruthfield

EXPLOSIVE REPORT ON SWALWELL ISSUED BY U.S. JUSTICE DEPARTMENT

Late today, the U.S. Justice Department announced it has in its possession a series of audiotapes which according to a highly placed government source, were retrieved from the home of Rep. Eric Swalwell (D-CA) after news broke about the congressman's alleged affair with a female Communist Chinese spy.

"The department has had this series of tapes for a number of years but chose to not release the information until now," said Case Officer Irving Lomein Noodleman who with several other officials held a press conference outside the famed Wai Yu Mun Ching restaurant in the nation's capital.

"Compromising someone was not on our menu," Noodleman added, "although we did place a recorder in

Ron Ruthfield

Congressman Swalwell's dresser drawer where he kept his drawers back in 2013, the year he was elected to serve the people living in the 15th District of Californication – sorry, California."

News reports from the past week have indicated that Swalwell who grew up in Sac City, IA, (if I'm lyin', I'm dyin') had been involved romantically with Christine Feng, or Fung Fung in Mandarin, Fun Fun in Cantonese, and Kum Skrew Mi in English, after he became a city councilman in Dublin, CA, a 40-minute drive from the Bay Area where Rice-a-Roni and Nancy Pelosi are the San Francisco treats."

Feng, whose nickname is Peeking Duck, came to the U.S. as a student in 2011 and fled the country in 2015 after Swalwell was informed by the Justice Department that Feng was likely a spy and took part in fundraising for Swalwell who sits on the House Permanent Select Committee on Intelligence and Asian and Chinese Delicate Dishes, including Sum Yung Chick.

Noodleman played one of the tapes, which he said was recorded in one of the early years of Swalwell's political career.

"You want Bang-Bang Shrimp?" Swalwell asked her.

"Why you call me shorty? Sure, I want bang-bang but I no tiny person," Feng answered on the tape, adding, "I five-feet-one-inch, no shrimp."

"No, Feng. You don't understand. I was asking you what you like to eat because we're going to San Francisco's Chinatown for dinner."

"Oh, you funny, Mr. Swellwell," she said as she gently rubbed his right thigh as she admitted on the recording, she was attempting to seduce him.

Ron Ruthfield

"Swalwell. Not Swellwell," he responded.

Despite the audio evidence, Rep. Swalwell maintains there was never anything between him and Ms. Feng, adding, "Not even an overstuffed egg roll."

Ron Ruthfield

THE ART OF THE HUNTER

As you likely know, Hunter Biden, son of the President of the United States, has become a much-celebrated artist and is on track to become as famous as his father, America's legendary b------t artist.

Do you also know that some of his Da Vinci-like "masterpieces" (I'm referring to Brooklyn's Guido Da Vinci who was a well-known forger of artwork and currency for the Gambino crime family) displayed in a gallery in the SoHo neighborhood of Manhattan came woefully close to a brush with a paint can over the weekend?

News reports say that a man wielding a container of spray paint (the color was unidentified, although one witness said it appeared to be Chinese Red) darted into the gallery and began to spray "Daddy" on the walls, apparently referring to the "Big Guy" now in the oval office of the White House. Close by were works by Hunter but fortunately they all escaped the crimson nozzle. "Bad aim," said one NYPD investigator who canvased

Ron Ruthfield

the canvases after they dragged off the pernicious pigment perpetrator. "Wouldn't want to see this guy on a gun range or on my paintball team."

The attempted vicious assault on an inspirational and majestic artistic piece created by Hunter Biden was second only to the nefarious incident that even came close to the near disaster quite recently. It was in 1972, the same year Joseph Biden was elected to the U.S. Senate, when some Hungarian lunatic by the name of Lazlo Toth decided to attack Michelangelo's brilliant statue of the Pietà, housed in St. Peter's Basilica in the Vatican, with a geologist's hammer and claiming he was Jesus Christ risen from the dead. Come to think of it, where else would he be?

To date, after a decades-long review, investigators have not been able to link the two events although in recent months U.S. Catholic Bishops are considering an official ex-communication of the current president and have taken into account the 49 years since President Biden has at certain times also claimed he was a savior. Coincidence? You decide.

After spending less than a week in a Rome mental hospital, Toth was released and quickly deported to Hungary where he opened a pizzeria until he choked to death as a result of sprinkling two pounds of paprika and an economy-size can of anchovies on one skinny slice and consumed it. At least that was the theory promulgated by the area's Catholic diocese but never proven despite the food storage section of St. Stephen's Basilica in the capital city containing two ocean-going shipping containers filled with mammoth fishing nets and a red, powdery condiment derived from dried peppers which easily could have been used by the entire population of Eastern

Ron Ruthfield

Europe, including Moldova, until the 22nd century A.C.E. which is a great card to be dealt in a game of blackjack.

Once the NYPD completed its initial investigation at the SoHo gallery, I called one of my confidential sources, a former curator for the Guggenheim Museum and asked him to go to the gallery to see what he could find out what was defaced. A couple of hours later he called back.

"I'm at the gallery and want you to know that none of Hunter's work was disturbed. Further, he has a really unique way of painting. He sticks a straw in his mouth and blows different color inks onto various surfaces, such as canvas, metal, and other substrates that absorb the various colors of ink. Quite colorful, actually, especially for a little girl's bedroom or the lobby of a Ukrainian gas company."

"The only thing I was ever aware of," I responded was that "I thought he only used a straw to either drink a Coke or snort some coke at the same moment. Man, that's some talent."

My contact added, "I was told by the gallery owner whom I've known for years that he wanted Hunter to send someone to pick up his art pieces and take them out of the gallery because he feared there would be more incidents. Lo and behold, about two hours later, up drives Hunter's newish Jewish bride, Melissa, in the family vehicle, packed it with the art, then took off heading south.

"Indeed, someone even remarked to me, 'Look at that Hunter van go'. And don't worry, I'll let you know everything I find out by keeping one ear on future events."

Ron Ruthfield

THAT CHAMPIONSHIP YEAR

In a most unusual move, the Federal Election Commission (FEC) held a press conference this afternoon to let American citizens know that the 2020 presidential voting will not take place on November 3 as previously scheduled.

Instead, the spokesperson said, the voting will be substituted with a 15-round boxing match between the candidates refereed by Congressperson Gerald Nadler (D-NY) who, in an air of fun and frolic, has agreed to be the third man in the ring. Nadler was officially entered into the World Boxing Council's Lightweight Division shortly after his last lap-band surgery.

The congressman, who sometimes uses the name Samson, was not at the FEC's presser. According to government operatives, he was spotted in the Congressional gym preparing for the bout wearing a surgical mask and rubber gloves while gasping for air on a rowing machine.

Ron Ruthfield

The commission's representative emphasized the agency has issued an order to governors of all 50 states that mail-in ballots – legal, semi-legal, somewhat legal, quasi-legal and patently illegal – will be officially tossed except for those who cast their votes for Kanye West whose base of voters has been hand-picked by the entire Kardashian family, including Bob, who suddenly died 17 years ago after hearing that OJ Simpson was actually guilty of killing his wife, Nicole, and her friend, Ron Goldman.

"Under normal conditions, the FEC oversees only the financial activities of elections but in this case, we are usurping our own authority by stepping in to ensure a fair fight between the candidates," the mouthpiece stated. "We anticipate hundreds of lawsuits as a result of the change, but we'll simply take the money to defend our position out of the campaigns' contributions coffers to pay for legal counsel who will include Michael Cohen, Rudy Giuliani, and Louis Farrakhan."

Instead of the usual nationwide voting, President Trump who is undefeated in one match, and two-time presidential candidate with a 2-0 record, Joe "Come-on-Man" Biden, will square off in the boxing competition to determine who will run the nation into the ground for the next four years even more than it has been. The venue and date have yet to be announced, although covert sources have told this correspondent that it's likely to be a Zoom event and will more than likely take place in the middle of the night in the men's locker room in front of the urinals at Trump National Golf Club in the nation's capital.

"Come on, man!" the ex-Vice President exhorted when informed he wouldn't be able to fight Trump in a Washington, D.C., schoolyard because of the ongoing problem with COVID-19 and the fact that Biden has never fought anyone

Ron Ruthfield

other than a six-year-old girl in gym shorts in a school playground. However, Biden admitted she knocked him out with a right uppercut to his chin.

"Trump is a lying 'paotesxi' (short for anything the president says) and he ain't black!" shouted Biden at the FEC spokesperson in an unusual outburst of mental cogency. The Assistant's Assistant Deputy Under Secretary of Protocol said that Biden had been invited to attend the flummery but blocked Trump from appearing because he was caught reading the Bible at a Cabinet meeting.

The FEC spokesperson temporarily remained unidentified while wearing a full-face covering, long sleeves, and gloves to protect her race and gender in an attempt to adhere to the new federal guidelines spelled out in the No-ID-Needed-For-Anything Act. It wasn't until after the press conference when the FEC emissary exposed herself by removing the mask she was wearing.

Biden stopped short of calling the FEC official a "junkie" but did take the opportunity to lick the spokesperson, former First Lady Michelle Obama, on her right ear lobe and attempt to cup her breasts with both hands. The gestures occurred just prior to her kicking the former Vice President in the groin, whereupon Biden fell to the ground and pleaded to go back to his basement bunker.

After Biden stopped crying, he appealed to the FEC representative to speak to Ukraine's President Volodymyr Zelenskyy to see if he could arrange for a Trump-Biden rumble in the conference room of Burisma Holdings office complex in Kiev. "I'll bring my son, Hunter, to make sure everything is above board and that the 'fix' ain't in," Biden said, just seconds

Ron Ruthfield

before CNN's Don Lemon who was covering the event called the candidate a stand-up American politician whose ethics replicate the "gold standard of honest diplomacy so obvious in many nations around the world, including Iran, Venezuela, and Papua New Guinea."

President Trump took the news in stride, according to White House Press Secretary Kayleigh McEnany. "The President said he was looking forward to having Michael Avenatti as his corner man considering the porn-star attorney became a professional masseuse after extensive training in rubdown and massage techniques from one of his clients, stripper Stormy Daniels, as well as from one of his cellmates."

"We think Biden's going to go down in the first round," McEnany added, "especially because Biden hates G-d."

"Besides, President Trump will have iron horseshoes stuffed inside his gloves."

Ron Ruthfield

THE MASKER AIDE

In my continuing effort to comply with local, state and federal mask mandates during the ongoing COVID-19 pandemic, I'm continually scouting for additional facial shrouds to conceal my mouth and nose.

The 117 cover-ups I already own are okay, but never quite seem fashionable enough (certainly not nearly like the 18-karat one being crafted in Israel embellished with 3,600 crusty diamonds that promises to light up entire skyscrapers in Tel Aviv if you tilt the cloth-covered glittering stones at the correct angle of the moon). Actually, that's the one at a price of $1.5 million, which has been ordered by a Chinese businessman from Wuhan living in the United States, although his birthplace has not been authenticated by any bats that I've flown into lately.

However, what I can corroborate is that in our thriving metropolis of Boone, NC – the center of the High Country

Ron Ruthfield

whose nickname is for obvious reasons – masks are now more common than dairy cows.

The other day, as I drove into the parking lot of our Walmart shopping center (actually, I was heading to the Dollar Tree to pick up a case of crispy pizza-flavored pork rinds and licorice-flavored Pringles, along with a 24-ounce Mountain Dew) I noticed a Mask World stand spilling over with masks for sale.

"Hi, there," I said to the young lady manning or womanizing the booth.

"Well, hi," she responded. "Y'all lookin' for a mask?" she asked as she stared at my eyes with great suspicion, considering I was wearing a pea-green surgical mask covered by a see-through plastic shield from the top of my head to below my chin.

I actually thought about saying, "No, I was really looking for a watermelon," but I stopped short after noticing she was wearing cowgirl boots and hat, a leather Western concha belt and holster carrying what looked like a loaded Glock 44 semi-automatic. (I used to think the right to bare arms meant you didn't have to wear a shirt in public but living in Boone purged me of that notion.)

"Well, yes, I am. Do you have anything a little different? I'd sort of like to make a fashion statement among my friends and colleagues," I said, demurely.

"Fashion statement? We ain't got none of them unless you wanna make one to order," she declared.

Ron Ruthfield

"Oh, are you a designer?" I queried, thinking I would get a smile out of her plus an offer of at least a facial covering that included some semi-precious gemstones as big as river rocks.

"Naw, just a country girl whose daddy was a dirt farmer while momma churned butter and brewed white lightnin'," she responded. "But I'm a Pentecostal Holy Roller and I make some purty ones with images of Jesus, Mary, Joseph, and my boyfriend, who's gettin' out of jail next week for sexually assaulting one of our cows.

"Just 'twan't fair of the sheriff to arrest him 'because he was wearin' his WuFlu mask, and I heard that Mad Cow disease wadn't around anymore so no need to worry about the cow. Two years waitin' for him wadn't bad. Gave me some time to practice my shootin', improve my mask-makin', and fool around with my first cousin, Elvis."

"Well, whatever you make me, I must have your word in writing that after you finish my face covering, you'll put it on, then spray yourself in the face with a chemical warfare agent to determine if it prevents pathogenic contamination," I insisted.

"Y'all are so funny," she responded. "All you Yankees make me chuckle. Any particular brand you want me to use?"

"Anything that's made in China will be fine," I said. "We're all going to have to get used to it, sooner or later."

Ron Ruthfield

GRAB A TWO-FER BEFORE THEY'RE SOLD OUT!!

With great alacrity, an unabashed hairless gremlin living in the White House (I'm not joking about thousands of them who now call the President's residence their home and rattle on and on and on only to be bitten by Commander, El Comandante's former favorite snack-attack mutt) has proclaimed throughout the land that the nation's Executive Mansion is being converted into a time-share operation run by Gov. J. B. Pritzker, (D-IL).

ALERT: The very same gremlin has announced that the canine cur has bitten so many people, causing several of the residence's employees to declare 100% disability most likely in an effort to reflect the image of the president, that they're moving him to a different undisclosed location. The dog, that is, not the president. He also said the German Shepherd will be dealt with by the Navy's crack seal team, knowing that seals have always had problems with Germans. One observer mentioned that he actually spotted a blow dart in Commander on the front lawn of the White House, perhaps propelled into his body to sedate him by a Washington, D.C. gang member, although it was reported that a black hood was put over the dog's head by the Secret Service so that man's best friend wouldn't be too frenzied.

Pritzker is a heavyweight (he once stepped on an industrial scale and a blinking neon light flashed on and off telling him he equaled the record weight of President William Howard Taft who once stepped on that same scale and registered 412 pounds) in the hospitality business.

The governor is no stranger to vacation ownership pads, especially because of his family's founding of Hyatt Hotels whose pristine record in the time-sharing industry only had to defend approximately 500,000 lawsuits just in Mexico alone for what buyers called, "The most perfidious, sniveling, conniving, untrustworthy business in our galaxy," and which was defended by the Pritzker family by telling time-share owners in a direct mail drop, "Ha, ha, ha, ha. The statute of limitations is way past due, sucker."

Oh, did I mention Pritzker is a progressive Democrat and is known as a jeunesse dorée, which in English means "I'm a fat-cat, brobdingnagian gazillionaire whose favorite patriot is Jussie Smollett, a fine resident of Illinois?"

The gremlin, whose name was given as one Hunter Biden by the White House Public Information Department, said that the prices would depend on which room buyers select as their vacation dwellings.

Ron Ruthfield

"For instance, (that's gremlin-speak for 'I'm lying') if a family of 14 want to occupy the Oval Office for one week during the summer, the cost will be a mere $3.5 million for a five-year period. Of course, that includes my commission of 20% and another 10% for the big guy.

"Imagine you and your family in the Lincoln bedroom or in the Residential Wing of the President's Palace for as little as giving us your children to raise until they're ready to join the Youth Arm of the Wingnut Party," he announced, knowing that the government needed to make room for illegal immigrants rambling through our nation and needing places to sleep like the West Wing which easily can accommodate 7,000+ (approximating one-half day's number of migrants crossing the Texas border) comfortably.

In the event you're wondering where the new White House will be, a Special Task Force is looking for an appropriate location in various foreign countries, including Bhutan.

(**Author's Note**) I'm a dedicated professional journalist and in all the years of reportage, I have *always* kept my principles of being fair-minded, honest and as lucid as possible, including the several times I was committed to a mental institution by various government agents and my first wife.

But that's not all. Mar-A-Lago, the home of former President Donald J. Trump, will also be converted into a time-sharing venue. Judge Arthur Engoron, presiding over Trump's civil trial in New York over the worth of Trump's real estate holdings, has declared that the sprawling Palm Beach complex is worth $18 million, a mere $900 million below what your average fourth grader can figure out if they've already graduated from the Wharton School of Business.

Ron Ruthfield

Following that, the fine judge, calling it a gag order, put his hand in his pocket, pulled out a handkerchief and forced the bailiff to stuff it down Mr. Trump's throat, making the head of the Trump organization's skin and hair turn more orange than they ever were.

And because of that definitively professional appraisal, time-share units will be sold at Mar-A-Lago for as little as $99 a week. The gremlin also said if you buy one at the White House and one at Mar-A-Lago, you'll get a 10% discount, adding, we do accept Visa, MasterCard and American Express. We are giving carte blanche to whomever wants to purchase them which will automatically make them members of the Diner's Club.

Asked by a reporter why the judge mandated the $18 million appraisal, the smiling and oh-so-witty Judge Engoron declared, "I was always taught to make up exact figures. And if someone asks where I got my information, I make that up, too."

Case closed.

Ron Ruthfield

HOME DEPOT AND LOWES BEGIN BATTLE IN UKRAINE

According to the latest insider executive and economics reports from America's two largest retail home improvement companies, it appears likely the two will be engaged in a continuing war by bidding against each other to secure the best locations in Ukraine's largest cities.

Home Depot and Lowes will be the only ones vying for properties in Kyiv, Kharkiv, Lviv, Dnipro and other major metropolitan areas that are presently considered villages, ghost towns, or cemeteries.

Despite objections by Ace Hardware, the place with the helpful hardware man, a spokesperson for the Ukrainian government stated that the company was actually too helpful to its customers and wasted too much time explaining do-it-yourself whittling projects when they could actually be shooting Russians.

Ron Ruthfield

Although retail outlets in Mariupol would have been commercial successes, asserted one insider in charge of government real estate acquisitions, there are no locations where Russian tanks can be parked without having to constantly shift forward and reverse gears, thereby causing traffic hazards that could result in fender benders in the entrance and exit lanes. In addition, there is presently not enough yellow paint to draw lines between spaces, especially ones reserved for the handicapped which now represents 82% of the Ukrainian population.

"We could actually purchase complete rubble and wasteland for a lot less in other Ukrainian venues, including boulder-littered parking lots. We simply want to show our compassion for all who have been involved in the conflict and not take advantage of rock-bottom prices being offered by the owners," revealed a person authorized to speak on behalf of one of the companies.

He added, "However, we have agreed to only raise existing prices on the products we sell globally by 20% to keep up with ever-increasing inflation trends caused by the strife, a move which was agreed to by President Biden."

Both corporations told the Ukrainian Defense Ministry they would continue to honor a 10% discount on all products for veterans who within another month or so will be 100% of their customer base.

Unofficial sources in what's left of the Ukrainian military said whichever company is chosen must, by contract, fulfill an obligation that requires the vendor to collect all metal, including bottle caps from vodka and beer cans within a 20-square-mile area of the retail sites. "Our workers will be given

Ron Ruthfield

professional metal detectors which most likely will reveal refrigerators, among other kitchen items, buried just beneath the surface."

"Those, along with flattened cars, children's bicycles, and steel beams from destroyed structures, will then be turned over to public and private arms manufacturers to be melted down and re-purposed into tanks, ballistic missiles, bullets, and Putinov cocktails for use in more and more war zones, including New York City, Kenosha, Wisconsin, and Myanmar."

"If any weapons or military equipment is left over, we will immediately ship them to the Taliban in Afghanistan," said a representative from the White House at the request of President Biden. "At least they'll be put to good use with the other armaments we gave them."

The biggest problem the companies face, according to Ukrainian President Volodymyr Zelenskyy and the Wall Street Journal, is helping us to repatriate the nearly four million citizens who took their permanent vacations in other countries.

Human resource personnel from both retail chains said starting wages will be reasonably high compared to other countries who have just been through wars. "The one caveat we agree upon is that Russians need not apply."

Ron Ruthfield

UN BLAMES ISRAEL FOR RUSSIAN AGGRESSION

In an overwhelming display of global solidarity, the United Nations General Assembly today voted to condemn the State of Israel for Russia's aggression toward Ukraine and what it called "Israel's invasion and interference in a member state's sovereignty, except for polar bears living on ice floes off the coast of Siberia."

According to Natasha Pelosky, former Squeaker of the U.S. House of Representatives, and Britney Spears, newly appointed U.S. Assistant Ambassador to the UN, "The United States is in lockstep with the rest of the world in denouncing Israel for its chutzpah in stirring the pot of beet borscht, a steamy recipe which has the Israeli delegation to the world body seeing red."

In the vote cast by 192 nations, only one gave its thumbs down against the measure, that being the representative from the Pacific Island nation of Kiribati, Teburoro Tito, who

Ron Ruthfield

claimed he had never heard of Israel "so why should I condemn it when I've actually attended a couple of bar mitzvahs in Fiji where they tossed me around in a chair until I passed out from too much Manischewitz wine?"

The more well-known Tito, Marshal Josip Broz Tito, was the former Yugoslavian revolutionary who once wrote to Joseph Stalin to "stop sending people to kill me" which is just about how leaders in Eastern Europe have been reacting to Vlad Putin for the past quarter century.

Tito the Slav abstained from voting on the UN issue considering he died 42 years ago. Somehow, according to reliable sources in Illinois, he still gets to vote in Chicago elections.

This latest UN vote sets a new record of blame against Israel that at the end of today's session reached a total of 6,651,001 ballots against the Jewish State since it gained independence in 1948 versus 12 – well, maybe 13 – against all other member nations during the same period of time.

They include those against Israeli Prime Minister Golda Meir, who was – bet you didn't know – was born in Kyiv, Ukraine, and who once boldly told the Russian ambassador to the world body while blowing smoke in his face from her 32nd cigarette of the day, "You might not like Israelis, but I can certainly kick your little red ass."

Spoken like a true Ukrainian, American, and Israeli patriot.

Ron Ruthfield

WHITE HOUSE ANNOUNCES BIDEN TO TAKE TWO, SIX-MONTH VACATIONS NEXT YEAR

Because of what the White House says has been a "grueling, hectic, and daunting schedule," President Biden will be taking only two vacations next year, each of which will be six months on the Gregorian calendar (named for famous actor Gregory Peck after he passed away in 2003).

"Limiting his trips, especially on airplane stairs, bicycles, and sandbags, will be easy," said the president's Chief of Staff Jeff Zients, who nobody in the United States, other than his parents and wife, ever heard of. Zients said his plan is to keep the president sedentary, a total reversal of the Commander-in-Chief's wildly peripatetic and turbulent itinerary which, at times, have put him to sleep while standing.

Ron Ruthfield

"We're also planning to install training wheels on his tricycle when we take him to the park and treat him to a vanilla ice cream cone once a week right after he watches morning TV cartoons."

"The American people know that the 360 days – five days less than a year in the event you weren't counting – President Biden has vacationed during his first presidential term to date were during what is considered to be one of the most formidable and arduous White House agendas since Rip Van Winkle fell asleep in the Lincoln Bedroom. That does not include his trips to each of the 35 bathrooms in the Executive Mansion."

"Note that the president still has about 89 months left this year to add to his government-authorized and taxpayer-funded vacation days, including Thanksgiving, Christmas, Veterans Day, his grandchildren's birthdays, Hunter's pardoning day, Rosh Hashanah, Yom Kippur, Columbus Day, and Donald J. Trump, Jr.'s birthday, which will bring his weekly average of holiday time off to six, not including overtime.

"Well, we're going to make certain that President Biden gets plenty of rest and relaxation," Zients added before telling the White House press pool, "Indeed, 'Sir Woke-a-Lot' as he's known by his colleagues, will be quite surprised when his cadre of Bidenomics experts put into motion an extra effort to quadruple the national budget, increase the federal debt by 98% per person which reflects the on-sale discount price – and market the event as the New American Spendamonia Marathon that includes the cost of 350 million tubes of hemorrhoid cream as authorized by the Internal Revenue Service. The president and his economic team are really bending over to ensure that all Americans will benefit from the ointment."

Ron Ruthfield

It's a bit early to predict which basement in which President Biden will be placed when the 2024 election season will be fully underway. But oddsmakers in Las Vegas and London are laying 10-to-1 that if Biden runs (a major feat for his feet) he will likely execute his original plan for his first term in office which thus far has worked perfectly.

"He will take steps to restore America's standing in the world, strengthen the U.S. national security workforce, rebuild democratic alliances across the globe, champion America's values and human rights, and equip the American middle class to succeed in a global economy," Zients commented, adding, "Nah, I'm just kidding."

According to 142 national surveys since the beginning of this year, President Biden has accomplished so much for the nation he'll most assuredly deserve another 720 days of vacation in his second term.

And at the age of 85 will finally be able to spend his final years in a 15,000-square-foot mansion on Martha's Vineyard to show the nation how much he has sacrificed for the future of American values and families.

Ron Ruthfield

SMOKE SIGNAL ANNOUNCEMENT: SENATOR WARREN ADMITS ORIGINAL HERITAGE

In a shocking moment of candor and clarity, Sen. Elizabeth Warren (D-MA) has announced that she is now a full-blooded Ukrainian.

"I base this on my ability to change my hair color from my present Uwodige (Cherokee for mousey brown) to shiny Odessa satin blond – all while doing the Hopak, the national dance of my war-torn nation," she insisted as two of her 150 senate aides slipped onion juice through a medicine dropper in her eyes to produce some tears.

"I've always believed flexibility is the key to success even if you change your mind 27 times a day," a habit which most people liken to someone with schizophrenia and drinks a lot of beer.

Ron Ruthfield

"Nobody should ever question my personal credentials again," Warren noted, adding that her great grandmother and great grandfather on her mother's side were born in a village called Chernobyl which, according to the official senate grifter, "still has tree-lined streets that light up 24 hours a day." However, a long-time rumor suggests that the enlightened senator who was a professor of law at the Jew-embracing Harvard University, is actually the illegitimate child of former Chief Justice of the Supreme Court Earl Warren.

Asked if she was planning to participate in any public anti-Russian demonstrations because of Putin's massive intrusion in Ukraine, she responded with a quick, "Nyet!" Although who can forget her speech less than a year ago calling for the overthrow of Benjamin Netanyahu, Prime Minister of Israel? "Aw, I was just joking about that," said the chuckling, grotesque, sloth that has the ability to snooker anyone with an IQ below 50 or a dozen dumb chickens.

For years, Warren proclaimed she was a member of the Cherokee Tribe until she was caught plagiarizing smoke signals and blowing them at a rival tribe, a cloudy move that branded her a permanent outcast in Native American history mainly because several words were misspelled (perhaps because of 35 mph winds) and mistaken for a Ukrainian dialect called "Kraponya."

Once known as Squawk-a-yenta, the senator claims she would never purposely appropriate another culture's symbols, language, or customs, except when running for elected office or simply sitting around her wigwam drinking a six-pack of 7 Clans Blond Ale brewed in Cherokee, NC; a double horilka which is Ukraine's national drink often used as a powerful

Ron Ruthfield

laxative; or a Black, White, Red, or Yellow Russian spilling over the rim of her samovar with homemade citrus vodka.

"In fact, even though I was Native American at the time, I still honored Ukraine and always will," she said during a recent emergency senate committee hearing on national security.

"I even played the Ukrainian bandura and my first husband, Jim Crow (which in Native American means "stomachache"), strummed a sopilka during our wedding ceremony at a traditional tribal festival catered by the Second Avenue Delicatessen near my hometown of Oklahoma City. They even served pickled herring, which of course is my maiden name." (**Editor's Note:** "Pickled" is not part of her maiden name but Herring is, as in Elizabeth Ann Herring (hold the sour cream). Seven hundred pounds were shipped in especially for the marital occasion from Odessa that sits on the Black Sea, also called the African American Ocean.

So far, there's been no evidence that President Biden has plagiarized Warren's plagiarism, but plagiarism lasts forever. Remember, there's still time to go in his administration, and Warren's head, loud mouth, and habitual lying are bound to pop up like a cheap tent at the next Boy Scout Jamboree, if that organization is still in business and hasn't been taken over by pronoun-obsessed acidulous tyrants.

And tyranny is what Warren wants if we take her at her own word beginning with the filtered fact that she's definitely three teepees short of a powwow.

Ron Ruthfield

WHEN HAIRY MET NANCY

Ladies and gentlemen. The story you're about to read is true. The names have not been changed because we don't want to protect the guilty. (Dum, da dum dum.)

It was Monday, September 1st. It was cool in San Francisco. We were working the day watch out of Vice detail. My partner's Frank Smith. My name's Friday. Joe Friday. We were doing routine patrol downtown with our COVID masks on when we got a call about a possible break-in at a beauty salon. We rushed to the scene and arrived in less than five minutes.

"This could be dangerous," I said to Frank when I noticed the front door was wide open. "Yeah, I know, Joe." Frank was a man of few words, which is why his nickname was "Monosyllabic."

Guns drawn, we entered the front door of the business and spotted an elderly unarmed woman with a facemask draped around her neck. That was enough of a reason to order her to sit down in one of the swivel chairs even though she didn't have any arms.

"Why aren't you wearing your mask," I asked her, immediately noticing she had a soaking wet head, and her hair was covering half of her face.

"Don't you know who I am," the woman asked as she looked in the mirror in front of her staring at our reflection?

"No, ma'am, I don't, although you do resemble the Squeaker of the House."

"SPeaker of the House," she said with a certain boldness that sounded more like an insult. She looked in the mirror in front of her and blurted, "Yikes, I had no idea the color changed to orange. For a moment I thought my hair made me look like President Trump."

"No need for sarcasm, ma'am. Just trying to get the facts. All we're looking for are the facts. Doesn't matter to us what the color is, ma'am. We're just here to protect the citizens of San Francisco. That's our job, Ms. Squeaker. Just doin' our job, isn't that right, Monosyllabic?"

"Right, sarge," added my partner, Monosyllabic.

"SPEAKER," the lady screamed.

"Relax, ma'am. We got the call because beauty and barbershops aren't supposed to be open in our city by the bay. We're just trying to figure out why you're here and not wearing your mask. Even your stylist is wearing a mask. We've put people in Alcatraz for less than that."

Ron Ruthfield

"Well, because my hair stylist said I could come in for a wash and a blow, and that I didn't need to wear my mask inside the shop."

"Ma'am, that kind of language is uncalled for," I said. "It's people like you who abuse the system and spoil it for the rest of the decent folks in the city. Now, I'll need to see some ID."

"ID? Are you serious? Identification isn't even needed to vote so why would you want to see my ID?" she asked. "Anyway, I don't have my purse with me."

"Well, ma'am, how'd you get here?" I asked.

"My chauffeur, Congresswoman Alexandria Ocasio-Cortez."

"Yeah, I heard that name once. Is she old enough to drive?"

"YES," she said in a loud voice. "She's even driving the agenda for the Democratic Party. The Socialist arm."

I walked away for a moment to speak to Monosyllabic with privacy.

"I think we should let this go, Frank. Truth be told, she could also use a facelift."

"Wouldn't argue about that, boss."

I walked back to the chair and squawked to the Squeaker. "Don't let us catch you again without a mask on. The law says that Californians must wear face coverings when in public spaces, especially indoors and other areas where physical distancing is not possible."

Ron Ruthfield

"Of course, I know that," she snarled. "I ordered Governor Newsom to get that law passed but it excluded the rich and the powerful."

Nancy Pelosi was released after another warning that if she's caught again without a mask and identification, the consequences would be severe, including an official Training Course taught by Hannibal Lecter at the Harvey Weinstein Charm School.

AFTERWORD

I must impress upon you once more that COVID-19 was largely responsible for authoring this book. I mean, isn't that a natural reaction when someone is in a dreadful, pestiferous state of ubiquitous terror and angst?

Quite sincerely, I hope you enjoyed it despite perhaps some political, ideological and cultural disagreements.

This is the first edition of Satire for the Soul, and the second one is already being written even though the COVID-19 scare has somewhat calmed down. If you liked the read and there's a place you can review it and give it a five-star rating, please do. If you didn't like it, stay away from writing a review, and don't expect your money back any time soon.

Ron Ruthfield

www.ingramcontent.com/pod-product-compliance
Lightning Source LLC
Chambersburg PA
CBHW020310010526
44107CB00001B/56